THE POWER OF THE DALEKS
DAVID WHITAKER

EDITED BY JOHN McELROY

TITAN BOOKS
LONDON

DOCTOR WHO *THE SCRIPTS* : THE POWER OF THE DALEKS
ISBN 1 85286 327 7

Published by
Titan Books
19 Valentine Place
London SE1 8QH

First edition March 1993
10 9 8 7 6 5 4 3 2 1

British Library Cataloguing-in-Publication Data. A catalogue record for
this book is available from the British Library.

By arrangement with BBC Books, a division of BBC Enterprises Ltd

Typeset by Spectrum Typesetting Limited, London.
Printed and bound in Great Britain by Cox and Wyman Ltd, Reading,
Berkshire.

INTRODUCTION

The Power of the Daleks was arguably the most pivotal story in the entire
history of *Doctor Who*. When it was decided that William Hartnell was
no longer up to continuing his role as the Doctor, the obvious solution
was simply to cancel the programme, and replace it with something
entirely new. Instead, such was the public's affection for this still
relatively new science fiction adventure series that a decision was made
to re-cast the part of the Doctor, and to continue the series with a new,
slightly younger actor playing the title role.

Patrick Troughton was, of course, chosen for this onerous task, and
quickly succeeded in making the part of the Doctor his own. I can still
recall clearly the resentment I felt, as a child, when I watched the first
episode of *The Power of the Daleks*, and saw this impostor pretending
to be somebody he wasn't, but by the end of the story, I and millions of
other viewers alike, had come to accept that Patrick Troughton was
indeed the Doctor.

In studying the script during the preparation of this book, I came to
appreciate the subtle ways in which the viewer was unconsciously tricked
into accepting the new Doctor. First of all Polly and Ben, the Doctor's
two travelling companions, are deeply suspicious of the new Doctor,
even though they have witnessed the transformation with their own eyes
and within the confines of the TARDIS. Ben, especially, does not believe
that it really is the Doctor, and the Doctor himself merely adds to Ben's
suspicions by continually referring to himself in the third person. Ben is
finally persuaded when he realises that the Daleks themselves recognise
their sworn enemy. By mirroring the audience's initial distrust of the
new actor, and then allowing Ben and Polly to come to accept the new
Doctor, the viewer is cleverly persuaded to accept him as well.

Of all the stories that the BBC no longer has in its archives, *The Power
of the Daleks* must surely be *the* one that is most sorely missed. A few
years ago, when preparing the *Tomb of the Cybermen* script book for
publication, that story would have ranked just as highly. At the beginning
of 1992, however, it was miraculously recovered, and quickly released
by BBC Video for all to enjoy. Is it too much to hope that one day *The
Power of the Daleks* will also be recovered, so that everyone can enjoy

4 • THE POWER OF THE DALEKS

this magnificent story, not just in book form but in the medium in which it was intended to be seen?

My grateful thanks to Stephen James Walker for another informative background section, and to Jan Vincent-Rudzki and Stephen for their help in ensuring that the descriptions in the script are as accurate as possible. Thanks also to David Saunders and Gary Leigh for reference material.

John McElroy, November 1992

BACKGROUND

Transmitted at the end of 1966 as the third story of *Doctor Who*'s fourth season of adventures, *The Power of the Daleks* was a landmark in the series' history. Up until that time, the Doctor had always been played by William Hartnell, whose memorable portrayal of the character as a stern but kind-hearted grandfather figure, complete with long white hair and dignified Edwardian clothes, had endeared him to millions of viewers and helped to make *Doctor Who* the great national and international success it had become. In the first episode of this new story, however, viewers were introduced to a very different Doctor, played by forty-six year-old character actor Patrick Troughton.

This was by no means the first time a leading character in an important programme had been recast. Each of the BBC's three *Quatermass* serials of the fifties, for instance, had seen a different actor taking the central role of Professor Bernard Quatermass. However, whereas there had been a two or three year gap separating each of those serials, Troughton's début episode as the Doctor came only a week after Hartnell's finale.

William Hartnell had always been something of an eccentric, but during 1965 and 1966 he had become, by all accounts, increasingly cantankerous and difficult to work with. Having always regarded *Doctor Who* as primarily a children's programme, he had strongly resisted attempts by the production team to make the stories more sophisticated and 'gutsy'. He had also come to demand almost complete discretion to rewrite his dialogue and make other changes to the scripts, feeling that he understood the series, and in particular the Doctor's character, far better than the writers did. Moreover, due partly to ill-health and partly to the understandable strain of playing the lead role in a virtually year-round weekly series, he had become increasingly forgetful of his lines, causing many problems and delays during recording. In the end, the production team decided that they had little choice but to replace him when his contract next expired. Thus it was that at the end of *The Tenth Planet* - the story immediately preceding *The Power of the Daleks* - viewers saw the Doctor collapse to the floor of his trusty TARDIS and undergo a complete physical transformation - the process which in later eras of the series' history would come to be known as regeneration.

In announcements to the press, it was diplomatically suggested that Hartnell had left the series to resume his career in the theatre. Later, it was assumed that he had left mainly due to illness. His departure was by no means willing, however, and he was deeply hurt and saddened to have to give up the role of the Doctor. Fortunately, one thing of which he did approve was the choice of his successor. The series' then producer, Innes Lloyd, remembered discussing this with him: "I recall him saying to me - though I don't know if he said it to anyone else - 'There's only one man in England who can take over, and that's Patrick Troughton.'"

Although a number of other actors, including Sir Michael Hordern, were considered for the part, Lloyd regarded Troughton as "an absolutely ideal choice. He had versatility going for him - he was a distinguished character actor with a great many varied roles behind him. He was always in demand. He was a popular actor with a great following. Most important of all, I think, was that he had a leading actor's temperament. He was a father figure to the whole company and hence could embrace it and sweep it along with him."

Troughton was away from home on a film shoot when first approached to take on the role of the second Doctor.

"My association with *Doctor Who* began in Ireland," he explained in one interview. "I was there in 1966 filming *The Viking Queen* with Nicola Pagett when the phone started ringing. It was the BBC production office and they were looking for a replacement for Billy Hartnell, who was then a very sick man.

"'Come and play Doctor Who,' the voice on the phone said.

"'No, no,' I said equally emphatically, 'I don't *want* to play Doctor Who.'

"Anyway, the phone kept on ringing and I kept on saying, 'No, I *really* don't want to play it. It wouldn't last more than six weeks with me!'

"But they kept on phoning and pushing the money up, so that in the end I began to have serious doubts. After about a week of these calls, I decided I must be crazy to keep refusing. It was ridiculous. Even if it only lasted six weeks it was still worth doing."

In fact, one of the main considerations was the thought that the regular income would help to pay for Troughton's sons' education.

The weighty responsibility of providing the scripts for the new Doctor's début adventure was entrusted to one of the people who had been involved in the initial setting up of *Doctor Who* back in 1963: David Whitaker. Whitaker had been the series' story editor throughout its first year and had since contributed several stories of his own. He had recently been discussing a number of new ideas with the current script editor, Gerry Davis, and seemed a natural choice to tackle this important project.

The storyline that Whitaker came up with was entitled *The Destiny of Doctor Who* - a reference to the Doctor's transformation - and featured the series' most popular monsters, the Daleks. The hope was that the Daleks' presence would help to reassure viewers that this was still *Doctor Who* they were watching, even though the Doctor himself now looked different. Gerry Davis approved this idea and, on 22nd July 1966, commissioned Whitaker to write the complete scripts for the six part story, for a fee of £300 per episode. A separate fee of £15 per episode was paid to the Daleks' creator, Terry Nation, for their use in the story.

"This was around the time William Hartnell was leaving," Whitaker later explained, "and so, aware that the idea was to replace him with another actor, I wrote the Doctor's part as sketchily as possible, so that it could be easily altered. I then concerned myself with the rest of the story and delivered my scripts just before I was due to go abroad for a time."

Despite Whitaker's attempts to leave the Doctor's character undefined, Patrick Troughton found these initial scripts a source of some concern. To him, the Doctor came across as "a very verbose, autocratic Sherlock Holmes type - who never stopped talking!" Worried at the prospect of having to learn so many lines on a weekly basis, he felt that the character should be more of a "listener". *Doctor Who*'s creator, BBC Head of Drama Sydney Newman, also disliked the way Whitaker had characterised the new Doctor, suggesting that he should instead be a "cosmic hobo". This idea immediately appealed to Troughton: "I leapt at it! I said 'What a good idea!... A man like that'd be more of a listener, wouldn't he?'... I was very keen on the idea of doing it as a cosmic hobo."

Gerry Davis later described how the detailed characterisation was arrived at:

"We had to change the concept of the Doctor. We spent a whole day -

producer, Head of Serials, Patrick Troughton, myself and some others - at a meeting. As the morning went on it became chaotic. Everyone was giving ideas, but there was no real cohesion. I could see that Troughton was getting very irritated. He was very uneasy about taking the job anyway, thinking that he might be typecast. At the end of the morning I realised we were getting nowhere, so I ejected everyone else from the meeting and just Patrick Troughton and I worked out the character.

"Really it came mostly out of Troughton's own personality. In an odd sort of way he was playing himself. He was hard to pin down, shifting, always eluding the issue. This was very different from the positive, dogmatic character of Hartnell. So at the end of the day we went back and I said I thought we had it.

"I thought it would be very interesting to have a character who never quite says what he means, who, really, uses the intelligence of the people he is with. He knows the answer all the time; if he suggests something, he knows the outcome. He is watching, he's really directing, but he doesn't want to *show* he's directing like the old Doctor."

Davis was inspired in part by Destry, the character portrayed by film star James Stewart in the popular Western *Destry Rides Again*; someone who when asked a question would always reply by way of a parable rather than giving a straight answer.

Once the new Doctor's character had been worked out, David Whitaker's scripts had to be amended accordingly. As this was a last minute job, and as Whitaker did not have time to do it himself, Gerry Davis contacted another former *Doctor Who* story editor, Dennis Spooner, to perform the rewrite, beginning with the first episode over the weekend of 8th-9th October 1966. Spooner's fee for this work was £75 per episode. Whitaker agreed to the rewrite on condition that neither his own fee nor his overseas rights were affected, that the characterisation of the Daleks was not changed, and that he still received sole writer's credit.

"I rewrote the story from David's script," Spooner later confirmed. "Terry Nation had the rights to write all the Dalek stories, but he was busy and couldn't do it. So he handed the task over to David to write it. David wrote it as a straight piece for *nobody*. You see, he knew it wasn't going to be William Hartnell, and he didn't know *who* it was going to be. So he wrote it as 'the Doctor', and 'the Doctor' was really not written at all. Nothing the Doctor said was important to the development of the story. The Doctor was on the sidelines of the plot.

"When they cast Pat Troughton, Gerry Davis didn't feel that he, as story editor, could do the amount of rewriting that was going to be involved. As story editor, you've got to liaise with Make-up, Costume and all the other departments; you've got to look after your producer; you've got to take the director in hand. He knew that if he took this story, he would have to go home for three weeks to do the amount of rewriting it needed, so he asked me to do it.

"I went in and met Pat Troughton and I said to Pat, virtually, 'How do you see yourself as the Doctor?' That was obviously so I'd be able to write it as he wanted to play it. Basically, he saw it as Charlie Chaplin. So we went through it together, and his part expanded to just the right size. We were *enormously* over-length, because David used to overwrite terribly.

"It was difficult to rewrite the script for *The Power of the Daleks* because I had (a) to enlarge the Doctor's part in a script that was enormously over-length anyway, so it suffered badly, and (b) to eliminate a lot of sub-plots, some of which I was sorry to lose. There was one point where he had a very good sequence about a food machine, like the one on *Star Trek*, where someone dials up a meal and it comes out like a raspberry ripple ice cream. It was in the original Dalek story too, so it was lovely continuity, but the whole plot stopped for about ten minutes for this marvellous sequence with a food machine. I just *had* to knock it out."

When it came to choosing the costume and make-up that Troughton would wear, a number of colourful suggestions were considered. It was thought, for example, that he might black up and put on curly-toed slippers and a turban, or perhaps adopt the guise of a windjammer sea captain in full Victorian-style naval uniform. A number of ideas were actually tried out in costume tests, and each time Troughton was kitted out in a new look, Sydney Newman would be fetched to pass judgment. Newman's reaction was invariably negative and, as Troughton later attested, he finally asked, "But whatever happened to the cosmic hobo?" Consequently, Troughton's eventual costume, created by costume designer Sandra Reid, was a tramp-like, Chaplinesque parody of Hartnell's, with stove pipe hat, spotted bow tie, disreputable old frock coat and enormously baggy checked trousers.

At one point during the rehearsal process, Troughton reportedly proposed playing the part wearing a frizzy, Harpo Marx-type wig. In the end, however, his own hair was simply cut into a Beatle-style mop.

The director appointed to handle *The Power of the Daleks*, as it was eventually renamed, was Christopher Barry. Barry was a long-standing contributor to the series, having worked on the very first Dalek story amongst others, and he also knew Patrick Troughton of old.

"Patrick Troughton took to *Doctor Who* like a duck to water," he notes. "I don't think Sydney Newman was entirely happy with the first appearance of him during rehearsal. I think we had to tone it down a little, to try and incorporate more of Troughton's youth and humour and whimsy. Hartnell was always the old professor, grandfather sort of figure, which was good, but Troughton was a sort of whimsical figure, more musical, and advantage could be taken of that.

"Troughton, like Hartnell, was a very experienced actor and a very resourceful person. I think he found depths in his own personality. He nearly always played very straight, stern roles, like Cromwell in *A Man for All Seasons*, and I think he relished the idea of the Doctor. He was that sort of warm-hearted, lovely person himself, and it was seldom that he got a chance to play that sort of role in television. I'd worked with him both as a production assistant and as a director. I'd directed him in the BBC serial *No Cloak, No Dagger*, in which he played one of the murder suspects, a very monosyllabic Cornishman who was always a figure on the horizon watching and whittling a stick. I was delighted to be directing him again in his first *Doctor Who* story."

One of the standard dramatic functions of the Doctor's human travelling companions is to provide a point of audience identification in the stories, and this was certainly the case with Polly and Ben in *The Power of the Daleks*. Their initial astonishment at the Doctor's metamorphosis reflected viewers' own reaction to this radical development. Although Polly is prepared reluctantly to accept that the stranger they have found lying on the TARDIS floor is indeed the Doctor, Ben remains highly sceptical, suspecting that an impostor has infiltrated the ship.

It is only as the adventure progresses that Polly and Ben, and with them the series' viewers, come to realise that the new Doctor's clown-like façade masks a keen intelligence and highly developed powers of observation, and that the strong sense of morality which the first Doctor always manifested is equally apparent in his successor. Although his behaviour is rather more erratic and outlandish here than it would become in later stories, this provides an excellent early illustration of the second Doctor's characteristic traits and *modus operandi*.

The story's original writer, David Whitaker, did not altogether approve of the final version as reworked by Dennis Spooner. "It was a very different kettle of fish when it appeared," he later commented, "and I wasn't desperately happy about the whole thing." Terry Nation also disliked the story, although for different reasons; his main objection was to the one aspect of the script which Whitaker had specifically stipulated should not be changed by Spooner: the portrayal of the Daleks.

In Nation's eyes, Whitaker had depicted the Daleks as far less complex creatures than they had originally been conceived. This was a view that Christopher Barry shared. "*The Power of the Daleks* was my second Dalek adventure," he notes, "and at the time I did feel that they had changed from their first appearance. I know that I was always very critical about how they could and should work."

It must be said that such criticisms are not really borne out on objective consideration of the story. On the contrary, the Daleks are arguably seen at their most complex and devious here, lulling the gullible humans into a false sense of security by passing themselves off as humble servants whose only desire is to help the colony and improve the efficiency of its operations. Never before had their capacity for guile and deception been so vividly demonstrated.

The four Dalek props used in production of *The Power of the Daleks* were not newly constructed but assembled from a mixture of parts already existing from previous stories. The BBC Visual Effects Department did, however, replace all the existing eye-stalks and gun-sticks with new, slightly redesigned versions, achieving a uniform look. One of the four props was fitted with an electrically operated iris in its eyeball, so that it could appear to be focusing on its intended victims.

Recalling that the Daleks' ranks had been augmented in their début story with a number of board-mounted photographic blow-ups, Christopher Barry employed the same technique again. This enabled him to include a 'crowd' scene at the end of episode five, showing the multitude of Daleks which had rolled off a 'production line' set up inside the creatures' space capsule.

The production line sequence itself was achieved using both modelwork - with a number of suitably adapted Herts Plastic Moulder toy Daleks running along a miniature conveyer belt - and live action. One lightweight Dalek upper body section (minus both arm attachments) was constructed for the studio recording, where it was seen being lowered on wires onto a lower body unit, thus forming a (virtually) complete Dalek. These scenes also saw the use of a novel arm attachment, as one of the Daleks had its sucker cup replaced with a hemispherical scoop. This implement was used to carry the embryonic Dalek mutations from storage tanks to be placed inside their newly-constructed casings.

It was memorable sequences such as this which helped to make *The Power of the Daleks* a very popular story with the general viewing public, continuing the marked upward trend in ratings which had begun with *The Tenth Planet*. Averaging 7.8 million viewers per episode, it was the fourth highest rated story of the whole Troughton era. Its average position of 47th on the weekly TV chart was also the fourth highest achieved by any Troughton story. Today, it remains a very highly regarded production amongst the series' fans, although sadly it has not been seen in Britain since its original transmission, as no prints of the episodes survive in the BBC's Film and Video Library.

Stephen James Walker, November 1992

With acknowledgments to Innes Lloyd, Gerry Davis, Christopher Barry, David J Howe, Mark Stammers, Tony Clark and John Peel.

CAST

The Doctor .... Patrick Troughton
Polly .... Anneke Wills (1-3, 5, 6)
Ben Jackson .... Michael Craze (1-4, 6)
The Examiner .... Martin King (1)
Quinn .... Nicholas Hawtry
Bragen .... Bernard Archard
Lesterson .... Robert James
Janley .... Pamela Ann Davy
Hensell .... Peter Bathurst (1-5)
Resno .... Edward Kelsey (2)
Valmar .... Richard Kane (3-6)
Kebble .... Steven Scott (4-6)
Daleks .... Gerald Taylor (2-6)
                                                Kevin Manser (3-5)
                                                Robert Jewell (3-6)
                                                John Scott-Martin (4-6)
Dalek voices .... Peter Hawkins (2-6)
Guards .... Peter Forbes-Robertson (4-6)
                                                Robert Russell (5-6)
                                                Robert Luckham (5)

Extras:
Guards .... Tony Lammar
                                                Tony Leary
                                                Bernard Forest
                                                Victor Munt
Radio engineer/male rebel .... Philip Ryan
Male rebels .... Nigel Parry Jones
                                                David James
                                                Dave Carter
                                                Tony Rohr
Female rebels .... Nadia Baker
                                                Jenny Lautrec
                                                Jenny Robbins
                                                Judith Pollard
Dalek .... Nicholas Evans

TECHNICAL DETAILS

Story code: EE

Story title: The Power of the Daleks

Working title: The Destiny of Doctor Who

Authors: David Whitaker and (uncredited) Dennis Spooner

Number of episodes: 6

Studio recording dates: 22nd October 1966
29th October 1966
5th November 1966
12th November 1966
19th November 1966
26th November 1966

Studios: Riverside Studio 1 (main recording)
Ealing (film inserts)

Episode one
Duration .... 25'43"
First transmitted .... 5th November 1966, at 17:49:40

Episode two
Duration .... 24'29"
First transmitted .... 12th November 1966, at 17:49:14

Episode three
Duration .... 23'31"
First transmitted .... 19th November 1966, at 17:51:43

Episode four
Duration .... 24'23"
First transmitted .... 26th November 1966, at 17:49:33

Episode five
Duration .... 23'38"
First transmitted .... 3rd December 1966, at 17:51:32

Episode six
Duration .... 23'46"
First transmitted .... 10th December 1966, at 17:51:50

Episode six broadcast from film due to extensive editing.

PRODUCTION CREDITS

Producer	Innes Lloyd
Script editor	Gerry Davis
Director	Christopher Barry
Designer	Derek Dodd
Daleks created by	Terry Nation
Production assistant	Michael E Briant
Assistant floor manager	Marjorie Yorke
Assistant	Gail Paul
	Sybil Harper
	Jennifer Jones
Vision mixers	Clive Doig
	Dennis Curran
Floor assistant	Julian Aston
	Eddie Shah
Sound	Buster Cole
Grams operator	Lance Andrews
Lighting	Graham Southcott
	Ray Hider
Film cameraman	Peter Sargent
Film editor	Jim Latham
Costumes	Sandra Reid
Make-up	Gillian James
Incidental music	Tristram Cary
Special sound	Brian Hodgson
Theme music	Ron Grainer
	BBC Radiophonic Workshop
Title sequence	Bernard Lodge

EPISODE ONE

1. INTERIOR THE TARDIS.

(THE DOCTOR lays unconscious on the floor, his face partially obscured by a strange glow. As POLLY and BEN look on, helpless, the glow begins to fade, and they look at each other in horror as they realise that the figure before them is no longer that of THE DOCTOR.)

POLLY: Ben... his face... look at it!

BEN: He's breathing...

(BEN turns to look at the TARDIS console, and then looks around the control room.)

... and the TARDIS seems to be normal.

(POLLY is still staring down at THE DOCTOR. She goes to touch him, then changing her mind, pulls her hand back, obviously scared.)

POLLY: Ben, what are we going to do? We can't just leave the Doctor there.

BEN: Him? The Doctor?

POLLY: Well that's who came through the doors. There was no-one else outside.

                (BEN *considers this, and looks first at the closed doors of the TARDIS and then down at the body on the floor.*)

                Ben, do you remember what he said in the tracking room? Something about... "this old body of mine is wearing a bit thin."

BEN: So he gets himself a new one?

POLLY: Well... yes.

BEN: Do me a favour!

POLLY: Well, whatever happened, happened in here.

BEN: That's impossible!

POLLY: Not so long ago we'd have said that about a lot of things.

                (BEN *stares at* POLLY, *realising the truth in what she says. He looks around the control room, wondering at it anew. On the floor,* THE DOCTOR *groans.*)

                Ben!

                (BEN *turns, and follows* POLLY's *gaze down to* THE DOCTOR. THE DOCTOR *moves slightly and slowly opens his eyes.* BEN *and* POLLY *back away slightly, still unsure of the stranger before them.* THE DOCTOR *levers himself up with one hand, and suddenly clutches his head as he hears a jangling of music inside his head, like a record being played too fast. With an effort he tries to focus on* BEN *and* POLLY, *and cries out loud.*)

THE DOCTOR: Slower... slower...

(THE DOCTOR *groans as if in great pain.* BEN *and* POLLY *watch, fascinated, but at the same time scared. The music inside* THE DOCTOR'*s head finally begins to abate, and he rocks back and forth, still holding his head.*)

Concentrate on one thing... one thing.

(THE DOCTOR *turns and stares at the control console, as if trying to concentrate his senses. Slowly he takes his hands away from his head, and his face brightens in relief.*)

It's over! It's over!

BEN: Doctor?

(THE DOCTOR *scrambles to his feet and, still slightly unsteady, leans across the console. He operates the controls and the familiar sound of dematerialization is heard. The time-rotor starts its steady rise and fall.* POLLY *and* BEN *watch all this in silence, not daring to speak. They exchange nervous glances, and finally* BEN *moves forward and tentatively speaks.* THE DOCTOR, *without turning to look at* BEN, *reacts to the word "Doctor". His hands move to his face to feel it, as if seeking confirmation as to whether he is* THE DOCTOR *or not any more. Dissatisfied at this type of examination, he looks around and sees a storage chest, which he goes over to. He is hampered by the long, loose cloak he is wearing and he unties it, letting it drop to the floor, where he kicks it away. The clothes* THE DOCTOR *is wearing are several sizes too big for him and they are shapeless and baggy. In his*) *struggle with the cloak, the ring on his finger falls off and clatters to the floor. He doesn't seem to notice, and moves towards the chest, walking with some difficulty and again muttering to himself.)*

THE DOCTOR: The muscles are still a bit tight.

(POLLY moves forward and picks up the ring. BEN moves over to POLLY and stares at THE DOCTOR as he rummages through various souvenirs and other items picked up on past travels. THE DOCTOR exclaims gleefully and proceeds to stuff them all into the many pockets of his jacket.)

BEN: What are we going to do?

POLLY: It is the Doctor... I know it is... I think.

BEN: It's not only his face that's changed... he doesn't even act like him.

(BEN takes a breath and, pulling himself up to his full height, speaks with determination.)

Come on. It's time we sorted this out.

(He moves across to THE DOCTOR, POLLY following with considerable apprehension. THE DOCTOR is still busy, filling his pockets with all manner of items. As BEN approaches, THE DOCTOR finds a mirror.)

Now look here...

THE DOCTOR: Hold that!

(THE DOCTOR thrusts the mirror into BEN's hand, and stares into it.)

Tilt it.

(BEN *reluctantly does so. As* THE DOCTOR *looks into the mirror, suddenly, for a moment, the reflection seems to be of his old self. Then just as suddenly the image changes to a true reflection of his new self.* THE DOCTOR *makes an approving sound and turns back to the storage chest.*)

BEN: Have you done with this?

(THE DOCTOR *glances at the mirror* BEN *is offering him, opens a pocket or two and, realising that he cannot fit much more in his pockets, waves a dismissive hand at it.*)

THE DOCTOR: Put it down... put it down.

BEN: Now what's the game, eh?

(THE DOCTOR *turns to look at him, an ornamental dagger in his hand.*)

THE DOCTOR: From the crusades... from Saladin. The Doctor was a great collector, wasn't he?

(*The dagger vanishes into another pocket, and* THE DOCTOR *once again turns back to the chest.*)

POLLY: But you're the Doctor!

THE DOCTOR: Oh, I don't look like him.

BEN: Who are we?

THE DOCTOR: Don't you know?

(THE DOCTOR *has taken out a piece of dull metal. As he looks at it, he remembers something, and all the mischief and glee fades from his face. He stares at it as recollections flood back.*)

Extermination.

(BEN *and* POLLY *look at each other nervously, at this sudden change, but just as suddenly it fades.* THE DOCTOR *pockets the piece of metal and gives a loud cry as he sees what is clearly the object of his search, a large magnifying glass. He snatches it up and begins to study his hand with great intensity.*)

Ah... very good... nails need growing.

(BEN *takes* THE DOCTOR'*s ring from* POLLY *and offers it to* THE DOCTOR.)

BEN: Now look, the Doctor always wore this. So if you are him it should fit now, shouldn't it?

(BEN *slips the ring onto* THE DOCTOR'*s finger. It is far too big.*)

There, that settles it.

(THE DOCTOR *chuckles at* BEN'*s stern, accusing face.*)

THE DOCTOR: I'd like to see a butterfly fit into a chrysalis case after it's spread its wings.

POLLY: Then you did change!

THE DOCTOR: Life depends on change... and renewal.

BEN: Oh so that's it, you've been renewed, have you?

(THE DOCTOR *ignores* BEN'*s obvious sarcasm and turns away, talking to himself, suddenly very serious.*)

THE DOCTOR: I've been renewed, have I? That's it, I've been renewed. It's part of the TARDIS. Without it I couldn't survive.

(POLLY *and* BEN *exchange glances behind* THE DOCTOR'*s back. Suddenly, he whirls round and faces them.)*

Come here! Come here... the Doctor kept a diary, didn't he?

POLLY: Yes.

THE DOCTOR: Thought so, I wonder where... I wonder where?

(He moves off and once again starts ransacking the storage areas, pocketing yet more things with almost childish pleasure. BEN *and* POLLY *watch, not knowing quite what to do.)*

POLLY: It's a very different Doctor, Ben...

BEN: Yeah, maybe... just where do *we* stand, though?

*(*THE DOCTOR *finds a recorder and, pulling it out, puts it to his mouth and starts to tootle a tune. He then stops, and seeing the diary he has been looking for, picks it up and starts to read.)*

POLLY: Doctor... Doctor, what's going to happen to us?

*(*THE DOCTOR *looks blankly up at her, as if he does not understand the question.)*

THE DOCTOR: I think... I think we must have landed for some time. I think it's time we went for a stroll.

(He looks over to the by now stationary control column and, still reading the diary, flicks the door control. The doors open and THE DOCTOR, *his nose still in the diary, moves towards them.)*

POLLY: But you don't know where we've landed!

BEN: No, and you haven't checked the oxygen... the temperature... or anything.

(THE DOCTOR *turns another page and mutters as he starts to exit.*)

THE DOCTOR: Oxygen density 172... radiation nil... temperature 86... strong suggestion of mercury deposits. Satisfied, Ben... now are you two coming or are you not?

(*He disappears out of the doors.*)

POLLY: He does know us! He said "Ben", didn't you hear him?

BEN: Yeah, I heard. But he might just have been copying you though, mightn't he?

(POLLY *frowns, once again uncertain.*)

2. THE MERCURY SWAMP (DAY).

(*The rocks are a kind of silvery colour, having long been sprayed by the founts of mercury from once-active geysers. One geyser still operates, if fitfully, sending up little spurts of silver drops from time to time. There is a slight mist here and there, adding a mysterious appearance to this unusual place. By the pool, from the rocks, occasional little jets of steam issue.* THE DOCTOR *comes into view. He still has his face buried in the diary. In front of him is a small pool, and he walks straight towards it. When he reaches the very edge of the pool, he stops and turns another page of his diary. Then, while still reading, he carefully walks round the pool until he is on course again. He takes several steps, looks up from the diary to consider something, and nods. Then he turns, looks back to the pool he has just navigated, and laughs as though it had almost plotted against him. His laughter suddenly dies away however, when he looks down and realises that he is now standing in another smaller pool of water, and the water is beginning to seep through his boots. He steps out of the pool, with an annoyed look, then seeing the funny side, moves on, thrusting the diary into one of his pockets. He calls back to* POLLY *and* BEN.)

THE DOCTOR: Are you coming, you two?

(THE DOCTOR *spots a medium-sized rock, jutting out into his path. He moves forward, a cunning look on his face. He pats the rock and chuckles to himself. He reaches deep down into one of his pockets and produces a tape measure. He measures the rock with growing delight, and is clearly satisfied. He taps his leg and mutters to himself.*)

Time I put you through some tests, I think.

(*He pockets the tape measure and turns, moving back a few paces. Then, observing the rock with one eye closed, he runs at it and successfully leapfrogs over it. As he lands, a man moves into view on the other side of the rock, wearing a futuristic space tunic.* THE DOCTOR *has landed in a crouching position and is not immediately seen.*)

EXAMINER: Hello? Hello, is there anyone there? Hello?

(THE DOCTOR *remains crouching down, and peers over the rock at the newcomer.* THE EXAMINER *shakes his head, looks all round, but does not spot* THE DOCTOR.)

Hello?

(*He gives up and mutters to himself.*)

Why don't they come?

(THE DOCTOR, meanwhile, has decided that the stranger is friendly, and stands up. As THE EXAMINER sees him, he moves forward, his hand extended.)

Ah, so you've come at last. I'm from Earth. I'm the Examin...

(THE EXAMINER's words are cut short by a gunshot, and he falls dead at THE DOCTOR's feet. THE DOCTOR, horror struck, looks down at the body, then starts towards the rock for cover. He stops, realising that he should give assistance, and looks apprehensively around, knowing that the assassin cannot be far away. He goes back over to the body of THE EXAMINER, but quickly realises that there is nothing he can do. THE EXAMINER, although dead, is still clutching some sort of circular badge and THE DOCTOR gently prises this from his hand. He reaches into another of his pockets and pulls out the wire-rimmed spectacles that the old Doctor used to wear. He puts them on and peers at the badge, but cannot bring its contents into focus. He takes them off and realises that he can read perfectly well without them. Feeling rather foolish, he throws them on the ground in disgust, but quickly changes his mind and, realising that they may someday be useful again, pockets them once more. He reads the badge out loud.)

THE DOCTOR: Earth Examiner... Accord every access... Vulcan...

(While THE DOCTOR is pondering the badge's meaning, an unidentified figure, dressed entirely in white, comes up behind him. As THE DOCTOR

bends down to look through THE EXAMINER'*s pockets for further information, the figure raises a white gloved hand, holding a pistol, which is pointed at* THE DOCTOR'*s back.)*

BEN (*oov*):   Doctor, where are you?

(The would-be assassin steps quickly behind a rock. As he does so, his gun hits the rock and THE DOCTOR *wheels round, his senses immediately alert.)*

3. THE MERCURY GEYSER.

*(*POLLY *and* BEN *are standing by the active mercury geyser and its pool.)*

BEN: Whoah! Init 'ot!

POLLY: Mmm. Do you think the air's like this everywhere?

BEN: No. Might be just around here. Don't want too many lungfuls of it, I know that. Yeah, when I was a kid, we used to live opposite a brewery. You could take a walk and get tipsy all in one go.

*(*POLLY *kneels down by the mercury pool.)*

POLLY: It's beautiful.

BEN: Don't touch it, Polly!

POLLY: I wasn't going to.

BEN: Quicksilver gets through the pores.

(He looks around for THE DOCTOR.*)*

Where is that Doctor or whatever he is got to?

(Behind POLLY, *a small jet of steam erupts. She*

turns her head, and the jet blows into her face. She coughs and starts to sag to the ground. BEN *sees what has happened and runs over to her.)*

What's the matter?

*(*POLLY *falls against him, unconscious.)*

Polly? Polly!

*(*BEN *looks around frantically.)*

Hey, Doctor... or whatever you are. Quick! Something's happened to Polly!

4. *THE MERCURY SWAMP.*

*(*THE DOCTOR *jumps up,* THE EXAMINER'*s badge still in his hand, as* BEN'*s frantic cry reaches him.)*

BEN (*oov*):   Quick! Over this way!

*(*THE DOCTOR *moves off towards the direction of* BEN'*s voice. As he goes, the white-suited figure suddenly emerges and strikes* THE DOCTOR *with the butt of his pistol.* THE DOCTOR *falls down, unconscious. The figure bends over* THE DOCTOR *and pushes a tunic button into his hand. Then the figure goes over to the body of* THE EXAMINER *and starts to drag it away.)*

5. *THE MERCURY GEYSER.*

*(*BEN *holds* POLLY *in his arms. He is about to move her further away from the geyser, when another jet of steam erupts.* BEN *staggers and falls, shaking his head. As he lays there, struggling for breath, the white-suited figure appears.)*

BEN: Doctor...?

            (BEN's last conscious sight is of the figure approaching him.)

            6. THE MERCURY SWAMP.

            (THE DOCTOR is still lying on the ground, apparently unconscious. Kneeling beside him is QUINN, a young man in his late twenties. As he examines THE DOCTOR, he turns him over and notices the large bruise on the back of his head. THE DOCTOR opens his eyes briefly and quickly shuts them again as another man in a white suit appears.)

BRAGEN: Ah, Quinn, there you are, what have you got there? My men found two more of them by one of the pools.

QUINN: This one's got a nasty bruise on the back of his head. Fallen over his feet and knocked himself out, I suppose.

BRAGEN: I suppose so...

QUINN: Why don't they use the kit we send them?

BRAGEN: Yes. The other two have had a rather bad dose of fumes. Well, the girl has anyway.

            (BRAGEN moves away. THE DOCTOR open his eyes, clearly concerned at this news of his two companions.)

QUINN: Girl?

BRAGEN: Yes... but she'll recover.

            (THE DOCTOR gives a quick smile and closes his eyes again. QUINN and BRAGEN turn as two men in white suits appear. One is carrying POLLY in his

arms, the other is helping BEN, *who has partially recovered his senses.)*

QUINN: These comic opera guards of yours do have some uses after all.

BRAGEN: I pick them for their physical fitness.

QUINN: I thought it wasn't for their IQ. Give me a hand with the Examiner, will you?

(QUINN picks up the badge near THE DOCTOR's *hand.)*

BRAGEN: I wonder why Earth has chosen to send an Examiner to Vulcan. Just now, I mean.

QUINN: I don't know.

BRAGEN: A mystery, isn't it? He isn't due for another two years.

(BEN starts to recover consciousness and coughs violently. QUINN *moves over to him.)*

QUINN: How do you feel?

(BEN shakes his head.)

We saw your rocket overshoot the landing area. Don't worry, most of the ships from Earth do overshoot. I'm Quinn, Deputy Governor.

(BEN does not understand what QUINN *is talking about, but fortunately is still too groggy to argue.* BRAGEN *moves forward.)*

BRAGEN: Bragen, Head of Security.

QUINN: Let's get them all back, shall we? I'll take the girl.

(He takes POLLY *from the guard who has been sup-*

porting her. BRAGEN *steps back, gestures to* THE DOCTOR *and* BEN, *and gives an order to the guards.)*

BRAGEN: Here, you two. Help carry the Examiner.

*(*QUINN *turns, and watches* BRAGEN *with a slight smile. He clearly does not think much of* BRAGEN. QUINN *turns and moves off. The look* BRAGEN *gives* QUINN's *back bodes ill for his future.)*

I suppose you Earth people can't wait to examine Lesterson's space capsule.

BEN: Eh?

(Two of the guards have lifted up THE DOCTOR's *body. His head lolls back, so that only* BEN *can see his face. He opens his eyes, smiles, winks at* BEN, *and closes them again.* BEN *stares at* THE DOCTOR, *unsure of what he is playing at, but does not say anything. They move off.)*

7. *LESTERSON'S LABORATORY.*

*(*LESTERSON *is a cheerful enthusiast, in his mid-fifties. A dedicated scientist. He is seated in front of a work bench, polishing a piece of metal. In front of him, on the bench, is an impressive variety of chemical apparatus, and behind him are various electric panels, full of switches and dials. But the laboratory is dominated by the presence of a space capsule. Behind the capsule is a window through which it has obviously been lowered. No opening in the capsule is visible, although the line of a door may be seen, near one of the fins of the power part.* JANLEY *enters the laboratory. She is in*

> *her twenties, slim and attractive. Her eyes reflect*
> *great character and determination.)*

JANLEY: Lesterson...

LESTERSON: Look at this.

JANLEY: They've just brought in an Examiner from Earth, and a couple of assistants.

LESTERSON: An Examiner? What's he here for?

JANLEY: I thought you'd know.

LESTERSON: It's the capsule... it must be. Well they can't stop me working on it, I'll tell you that...

JANLEY: Could anyone?

LESTERSON: The Governor's always been difficult about it. But surely they wouldn't have sent somebody all the way from Earth just to...

JANLEY: Look, what about the meeting?

LESTERSON: Meeting?

JANLEY: Yes, I've arranged everything. Can we still use the old rocket room?

LESTERSON: Yes, I suppose so. I do wish you wouldn't get mixed up with these pressure groups, Janley.

JANLEY: Somebody has to do something. The colony's running down and you know it.

LESTERSON: I'm too busy.

JANLEY: If we ran things, you'd have better facilities, more money. I wish you'd take an interest.

LESTERSON: Now look, I don't mind letting you have the use of one of my rooms now and again, Janley, but don't try to involve me.

(LESTERSON *holds up a piece of metal.*)

This is what I find important. Two hundred years in a mercury swamp, and this piece of metal is dropped from it. Look, a couple of minutes polishing and it's as good as new.

JANLEY: Wonderful.

LESTERSON: Rain, damp, heat, mercury... nothing touches this metal. No corrosion, Janley... think of that.

JANLEY: Well, I hope the Examiner lets you go on with your experiments. Frankly, I doubt it.

(*She moves towards the door.*)

I think the Governor's brought the Examiner here to stop you opening the capsule. You should join our group, Lesterson. You might need us one day.

(*She goes out.* LESTERSON *looks after her, his face lined with worry.*)

8. *THE REST ROOM.*

(THE DOCTOR *is sitting cross-legged on a bed, playing his recorder.*)

BEN: So the murdered man was the *real* Examiner?

(THE DOCTOR *blows several notes on the recorder and nods slowly. He then resumes his abstract playing.*)

Well, did you see who did it?

           (THE DOCTOR plays a single note and shakes his head.)

POLLY: The Doctor got this button though.

           (As she speaks she holds out the button that was planted on THE DOCTOR.)

BEN: Well, I think it's pretty dull around here. I don't know why we don't just go back to the TARDIS.

           (THE DOCTOR shakes his head again and plays a definite 'no' note.)

POLLY: Doctor, are you going to let them think you're the real Examiner?

           (THE DOCTOR nods mischievously and blows a couple of 'yes' notes.)

           Won't that be dangerous?

           (THE DOCTOR considers and then plays several more uncertain notes, which seem to indicate 'perhaps'.)

BEN: Look, why don't you stop blowing that thing and talk to us properly?

           (As he speaks, BEN reaches across and takes the recorder from THE DOCTOR, who mimes extreme hurt.)

POLLY: Ben!

BEN: Now don't you start... it's bad enough with him.

POLLY: He hasn't done anything.

BEN: Yeah, and that's just the trouble! He knows what happened back at the TARDIS, yet will he tell us?

Will he come out and say? Will he admit to being the Doctor?

(BEN *looks at the recorder in his hands and angrily blows a few tuneless notes on it.* THE DOCTOR *seems to find this amusing, laughs and curls up on the bed. A few moments later there is a knock at the door and* BEN *whirls angrily towards it.*)

Come in!

(*The door is opened by a guard. He and another guard stand by the door as* BRAGEN *comes in, accompanied by* HENSELL, *the Governor of Vulcan.* HENSELL *is a busy, forceful leader. Autocratic, brusque, a man well used to making decisions and delegating authority, of a minor kind. He is in his fifties.*)

HENSELL: I am Hensell, the Governor... I trust that you are all feeling much better.

(THE DOCTOR *reaches across and takes the button from* POLLY, *looks at it, and puts it in one of his pockets. He stands up.*)

BEN: I've felt worse mate. Er, Governor.

HENSELL: If Earth had seen fit to warn us you were coming, we might possibly have been able to guide you down to the landing area.

THE DOCTOR: If Earth didn't warn you we were coming, Governor, they must have had a very good reason.

(BEN *and* POLLY *look at* THE DOCTOR, *as it is the first time since his appearance changed that he has given a direct answer.* THE DOCTOR *covers this immediately by striking a very dramatic 'thinking' pose.*)

I wonder what it was?

(HENSELL moves towards him, his voice set.)

HENSELL: Now look here, I run this colony. I'm entitled to know why you have come to Vulcan. What is your brief?

THE DOCTOR: I am the Examiner.

HENSELL: Why are you here?

THE DOCTOR: To examine...

(He says this as if speaking to a backward child. Before HENSELL can react, THE DOCTOR claps his hands together in a business-like manner and continues.)

...and I intend to start my examination at once!

(THE DOCTOR goes over to BRAGEN and starts to examine his uniform, secretly searching for torn material. HENSELL quickly recovers.)

HENSELL: Someone's leaked reports about these rebel groups... that's it, isn't it?

THE DOCTOR: Your turn now, Governor.

(THE DOCTOR moves across to scrutinise HENSELL's uniform.)

BRAGEN: There is Lesterson's capsule...

HENSELL: Internal affairs are my business, Bragen. Please don't interfere!

(THE DOCTOR seems satisfied with HENSELL's uniform, moves back over to BRAGEN and studies his reactions as he continues to talk.)

THE DOCTOR: Please go on.

HENSELL: The capsule. It was found in a mercury swamp... It must have been here for centuries.

THE DOCTOR: Interesting... continue.

(HENSELL moves over to face THE DOCTOR.)

HENSELL: ...for centuries before the Earth colony arrived. I felt it might be dangerous, it might contain bacteria...

(THE DOCTOR looks again at BRAGEN, who returns the stare, somewhat embarrassed. THE DOCTOR nods and moves away.)

THE DOCTOR: I shall examine the capsule... later. You may leave us.

(THE DOCTOR lies down on the bed. HENSELL, not used to being dismissed in this fashion, tries to save face as best he can.)

HENSELL: I shall look forward to your report.

(He turns to BRAGEN.)

Bragen, see that the Examiner and his party get some proper clothes, will you?

(HENSELL and his entourage leave, and the door shuts. THE DOCTOR sits up, shocked, looks down at himself, then mutters in a somewhat hurt voice.)

THE DOCTOR: We are wearing proper clothes!

(The sound of the recorder starts up again. BEN looks across at THE DOCTOR, certain that he still had it. He looks at POLLY.)

BEN: Oh, how did he get that thing back again?

(THE DOCTOR *ignores him and lies on the bed, tootling idly on the recorder.* BEN *and* POLLY *move over to him.*)

That was a bit of a cheek, wasn't it? Seeing if the Governor was the guy that you got the button off.

(THE DOCTOR *continues to ignore them.*)

POLLY: Doctor?

(THE DOCTOR *looks up, and smiles encouragingly at her to continue.*)

When he was talking to you, you were staring at the other man...

THE DOCTOR: Yes, very rude of me, wasn't it? Terrible manners... To tell you the truth I was studying his reactions, seeing if he agreed with the story...

BEN: Did he?

THE DOCTOR: Must have a look at that capsule.

BEN: You know you want to watch you don't take this Examiner stuff a bit too far.

THE DOCTOR: Answers must come from that mercury swamp.

BEN: 'cos at least one bloke ain't going to be fooled.

THE DOCTOR: When Bragen found us... he definitely said space capsule.

BEN: Look, you're not going to fool the guy that did the *real* Examiner in!

(THE DOCTOR *has returned to his recorder, once again deep in thought.* BEN *looks at* POLLY *and shrugs.*)

9. *A CORRIDOR (NIGHT).*

(BRAGEN is busy pinning a notice up on a board. Near him are two guards. QUINN comes round the corner into view.)

QUINN:	Bragen? What's all this nonsense about having to have a pass to see the Examiner?
BRAGEN:	It's the Governor's idea.
QUINN:	Surely it doesn't apply to me?
BRAGEN:	It's not my order, Quinn. I expect the Governor wants to keep people away from him.
QUINN:	It sounded like one of your red tape ideas.
BRAGEN:	It has nothing to do with me!
QUINN:	Right.

(QUINN strides away down the corridor. BRAGEN watches him, then goes back to the board. As QUINN turns a corner, he nearly collides with JAN-LEY, hurrying in the opposite direction.)

JANLEY :	Oh!
QUINN:	Sorry, Janley.
JANLEY:	My fault.
QUINN :	Are you all right?
JANLEY:	Yes. Lesterson's just cleared me out of his lab. Is the Examiner going to let him open the capsule?
QUINN:	I don't know, I'm on my way there now. If I can push past Bragen's army of layabouts.

(QUINN *moves away*. JANLEY *watches him go, her eyes thoughtful*.)

10. LESTERSON'S LABORATORY.

(THE DOCTOR *is standing at the 'entrance' to the capsule, examining it with great care and thoroughness, frowning, and muttering unintelligibly.* HENSELL, BRAGEN *and* LESTERSON *are all watching him and exchanging occasional glances.* POLLY *and* BEN *are standing nearby.* THE DOCTOR *nods, chuckles to himself, then scurries across to the bench and picks up the piece of metal that* LESTERSON *had been polishing. He suddenly looks very worried and turns to* LESTERSON.)

THE DOCTOR: Where did you get this?

LESTERSON: It dropped from the capsule.

THE DOCTOR: Dropped?

LESTERSON: Yes, when it was being hauled into the laboratory. But look, you see? This metal could revolutionise space travel. That's why I am insisting that we open it. Who knows what other marvels there may be inside?

(QUINN *quietly comes into the room*.)

HENSELL: But Lesterson, I didn't think you could open it.

LESTERSON: Well I have a theory...

(*He crosses over to the capsule and taps the ridged 'entrance' area*.)

I'm convinced that the opening mechanism on the other side is either here... or here...

(He taps two points, one to the left and the other to the right of the entrance, each about half way up. THE DOCTOR *is still studying the piece of metal.* POLLY *and* BEN *watch him, puzzled, as he takes out the piece of metal he had in the TARDIS from a pocket and compares the two. He looks extremely worried.* THE DOCTOR *turns away.* POLLY *and* BEN *look at each other seriously.* THE DOCTOR *turns his attention to* LESTERSON, *who is busy expounding his theory.)*

Now my theory is that I can insert a laser ray in this ridge here. The ray spreads, fuses the opening device and gets us in.

HENSELL: Examiner, I shall have to make it your responsibility.

THE DOCTOR: A laser...

(He closely inspects the ridge through a large magnifying glass that he has produced from his jacket.)

Why not?

(He stares at LESTERSON, *who reacts uncomfortably.)*

It shouldn't be too difficult.

(LESTERSON picks up a laser torch and aims it to the left of the door. Nothing happens.)

LESTERSON: Well, we'll try the other side.

(He aims the torch to the right of the door. There is a crackling sound from within. He steps back. The entrance to the capsule opens. From the interior, the glow of lights can be seen. LESTERSON

hands the blow torch to BRAGEN. *Everyone crowds around the entrance as* LESTERSON *and* THE DOCTOR *enter the capsule.* THE DOCTOR *chuckles to himself.* POLLY *and* BEN, *looking quite bewildered, follow the others into the capsule.*)

11. INTERIOR THE CAPSULE.

(THE DOCTOR *and* LESTERSON *stand in a smooth-walled, empty compartment.*)

LESTERSON: Hmm. A bit... disappointing.

THE DOCTOR: Not really. This is just an entrance bay, isn't it?

LESTERSON: Yes, I suppose so.

(*He watches* THE DOCTOR *closely.* THE DOCTOR *moves to an inner metal wall and examines a thin opening in it, six inches long and a tenth of an inch wide. He tries to keep his excitement to himself.* HENSELL *and* LESTERSON *move in.*)

HENSELL: This doesn't get us very far, does it?

LESTERSON: Getting into the rest of the capsule is going to take time, Governor.

(BEN *has moved his way to the front of the small crowd.*)

BEN: Well, can't you use that torch thing again? There must be an inner door as well.

LESTERSON: I'd have to measure it up. And find out where the lock mechanism is.

THE DOCTOR: I think we'll leave it for tonight.

HENSELL: Leave it for tonight? What have we come here for?

THE DOCTOR: That is my decision, Governor.

HENSELL: Good heavens, man!

THE DOCTOR: Two hundred years you say this has been buried?

LESTERSON: At least.

>   (THE DOCTOR *moves out of the capsule.*)

>   *12. LESTERSON'S LABORATORY.*

>   (LESTERSON *follows* THE DOCTOR *out of the capsule.*)

LESTERSON: There must be something in the inner compartments. We shall be able to find out where it came from originally.

THE DOCTOR: It didn't come from this planet, Vulcan?

LESTERSON: Oh no, no, no. The metal is quite alien.

THE DOCTOR: Alien, yes... very alien.

>   (THE DOCTOR *looks at them all, as if suddenly aware of their presence.*)

Goodnight.

>   (*He abruptly leaves the laboratory.* POLLY *and* BEN, *a little surprised by this sudden departure, are left behind.* LESTERSON *and the others turn back to the capsule.*)

BEN: What's he up to now?

POLLY: Ben! We're not going to let him out of our sight.

>   (*They quickly leave the laboratory and follow* THE DOCTOR.)

HENSELL: Well, Lesterson, you've got your way. Was it worth

sending for an Examiner? This idiotic Examiner?

LESTERSON: I didn't send for him. I thought you did.

QUINN: Why don't you let me talk to the Examiner, Hensell. I can find out what he's here for.

HENSELL: No, no, no, no. You keep away from him. We'll leave him to work with Lesterson here. We've all got enough to do without having to worry about some amateur critic from Earth interfering.

QUINN: Five minutes...

HENSELL: You heard what I said, Quinn. You won't mind keeping the Examiner busy, Lesterson. I don't mind what you do with him, so long as you keep his nose... out of our business.

LESTERSON: Yes, all right.

HENSELL: All right, well we shall talk about it tomorrow.

(HENSELL *nods and he,* QUINN *and* BRAGEN *leave the laboratory. As soon as they have gone,* LESTERSON *turns and looks at the capsule. He smiles, goes over to the work bench, and realises that the piece of metal is no longer there. He looks worriedly towards the laboratory door.*)

13. THE REST ROOM.

(BEN *is resting on a bed, holding* THE DOCTOR'*s recorder.* POLLY *enters.*)

POLLY: Ben!

BEN: What?

POLLY: Ssssh! He's in the corridor.

BEN: Who is?

POLLY: The Doctor, you clod! Come on, quick!

                 (BEN *rubs his eyes and follows her out.*)

                 14. A CORRIDOR.

                 (THE DOCTOR *appears around a corner and moves off down the corridor.* BEN *and* POLLY *cautiously peer round after him and follow at a distance.*)

POLLY: He's going towards Lesterson's lab.

BEN: Of course... to that space capsule.

                 15. LESTERSON'S LABORATORY.

                 (THE DOCTOR *cautiously steps into the laboratory. It is deserted. He moves across to the capsule entrance and produces the two pieces of metal. He enters the capsule.* BEN *and* POLLY *open the laboratory door just in time to see the back of* THE DOCTOR *disappear inside the capsule. They move across the laboratory.*)

                 16. INTERIOR THE CAPSULE.

                 (THE DOCTOR *makes his way to the place where he earlier found the thin opening. He lifts the polished piece of metal and pushes it into the opening. It fits exactly. He chortles to himself, pleased that his deduction is correct. As he presses the metal fully in, there is a humming noise, and an inner door opens. Framed in the doorway are two* DALEKS, *covered in dust and cobwebs, their eye, gun and sucker sticks all hanging limply.* POLLY *grips* BEN's *arm, her eyes opening wide in amazement.)*

THE DOCTOR: Polly... Ben. Come in and meet the Daleks.

(The two companions move forward, somewhat embarrassed, realising that THE DOCTOR *has been aware of their presence all along.)*

BEN: The what?

THE DOCTOR: The Daleks!

POLLY: You could have opened this before!

*(*THE DOCTOR *gives her the two pieces of metal as he starts to examine the* DALEKS.)*

THE DOCTOR: These two pieces of metal are identical. The Doctor took one of them from the Daleks himself.

*(*BEN *moves forward, touching one of the lifeless* DALEKS.)*

BEN: Why do you keep saying "the Doctor" if you mean you?

*(*THE DOCTOR *is too engrossed with his find to hear.)*

THE DOCTOR: I knew I should find them here, I knew it!

BEN: They look 'armless... not very lively.

*(*THE DOCTOR's *eyes flick towards* BEN, *showing him that he has heard him.)*

POLLY: What do you think? Two hundred years in a swamp and you wouldn't look very lively either. Nothing could live through that, could it?

BEN: Live?

THE DOCTOR: Nothing human... no.

                (THE DOCTOR continues his examination.)

POLLY: Doctor, look.

BEN: What's the matter?

                (POLLY has seen something on the floor. THE DOCTOR bends down and examines the dust on the floor.)

THE DOCTOR: Then there were *three* Daleks in here. What happened to the other one?

                (Behind THE DOCTOR, in the shadow of the inner compartment, a strange, horrifying octopus-like appendage edges into view. BEN sees it first, and for a moment he is unable to take in the horror of what he is seeing. He manages a strangled whisper.)

BEN: Doctor!

                (THE DOCTOR turns slowly, and takes in the full horror of what BEN is staring at. POLLY screams.)

EPISODE TWO

1. INTERIOR THE CAPSULE (NIGHT).

POLLY: Doctor, look!

BEN: What's the matter?

(POLLY has seen something on the floor. THE DOCTOR bends down and examines the dust on the floor.)

THE DOCTOR: Then there were *three* Daleks in here. What happened to the other one?

(Behind THE DOCTOR, in the shadow of the inner compartment, a strange, horrifying octopus-like appendage edges into view. BEN sees it first, and for a moment he is unable to take in the horror of what he is seeing. He manages a strangled whisper.)

BEN: Doctor!

(THE DOCTOR turns slowly, and takes in the full horror of what BEN is staring at. POLLY screams. The creature scuttles through a gap between the wall and the floor.)

THE DOCTOR: Get me a light... there's a torch outside.

BEN: Did you see it?

THE DOCTOR: Quickly Ben, quickly!

        (BEN *goes to get the torch.*)

POLLY: What was it?

        2. LESTERSON'S LABORATORY.

        (BEN *hurries out of the capsule and goes over to the bench, where he sees an electric bulb connected to a long lead. He switches it on and off again, to test it, and starts to move back towards the capsule. As he enters the capsule, a man comes into the laboratory and sees where* BEN *is going. He pauses, and then leaves the laboratory.*)

        3. INTERIOR THE CAPSULE.

        (POLLY *is glaring at* THE DOCTOR, *who has clearly been ignoring her questions.*)

POLLY: Why don't you answer me?

        (BEN *enters with the light.* THE DOCTOR *quickly takes it from him and moves cautiously towards the place where the creature disappeared.* BEN *edges after him, motioning* POLLY *to stay where she is.*)

BEN: It was a sort of disembodied hand, like a claw... it was 'orrible.

        (THE DOCTOR *explores the area, but cannot find anything.*)

THE DOCTOR: No, nothing!

        (*He moves back to the two dormant* DALEKS, *shin-*

ing the light on the floor, where a circle of dust can clearly be seen.)

BEN: You're right... there were *three* Daleks.

POLLY: Do you know what it was?

(THE DOCTOR stares at POLLY, but doesn't answer. He shines the light down at the floor again as he notices something else.)

THE DOCTOR: Think. Think. Think.

POLLY: If there were three... who moved it?

(THE DOCTOR exits, leaving POLLY and BEN behind.)

BEN: Don't ask me... Lesterson?

POLLY: But he hadn't opened the capsule...

BEN: Oh, he *said* he hadn't opened it... let's get our facts straight.

THE DOCTOR (*oov*): Ha ha! Excellent. Good thinking. Good thinking!

(POLLY and BEN exchange glances and also leave the capsule.)

4. LESTERSON'S LABORATORY.

(THE DOCTOR is moving round the laboratory, examining everything. If there is a microscope, he looks down it, if there is a test-tube, he holds it to the light, if there is a piece of paper, he examines it, all with extreme thoroughness. BEN and POLLY appear in the doorway of the capsule and move to join him.)

BEN: Well, does that mean you think he's been inside?

THE DOCTOR: If he's been experimenting on the Dalek... Aha!

               (He sees something else and rushes to look. POLLY
               and BEN *follow.)*

POLLY: But they're things. I... I... I mean... they must be!

               (THE DOCTOR *spins around and brings up the light
               which he is still carrying. He holds it to her face,
               which glows eerily in the beam. He releases the
               button and the light goes out.)*

THE DOCTOR: This light is dead now... but watch!

               *(He presses the button again and the light comes
               on.)*

BEN: You mean these things just need power?

THE DOCTOR: Lesterson's a fanatic. The Governor's jealous of his
               own position...

               *(He sees another item worthy of his attention and
               darts over to investigate.)*

               ... what does that suggest to you?

BEN: I don't know... I hadn't thought about it.

THE DOCTOR: That all is not well in the colony. Add to that... a
               Dalek!

BEN: Blimey, you don't half make mountains, don't you?
               One Dalek?

THE DOCTOR: Yes! All that is needed to wipe out this entire colony!

               5. THE REST ROOM.

               *(The room is in semi-darkness, illuminated only by
               a concealed wall light.* QUINN *enters, at first*

unable to see clearly in the gloom.)

QUINN: Examiner? Examiner?

(He goes over to the nearest bed and switches on the bedside light... and sees that the room is empty. At that moment the door opens and BRAGEN enters, giving QUINN quite a shock.)

Bragen, don't you ever knock before you enter a room?

BRAGEN: I'm sorry if I disturbed you. I was expecting to find the Examiner here... not you, Quinn.

QUINN: Well he's not here. You'll probably want to start snooping under the beds... so I'll leave you to it.

(He abruptly goes to leave the room, but is blocked by BRAGEN.)

BRAGEN: One moment.

QUINN: Don't try your luck with me, Bragen.

BRAGEN: On the contrary, I'm trying to avoid trouble. The Governor gave express instructions that you were not to contact the Examiner. I find you here. I'm sure you can offer some suitable explanation...

QUINN: I can... but not to you.

BRAGEN: Before you go...

(QUINN seizes hold of BRAGEN's arm and flings him roughly to the floor.)

QUINN: Don't ever try to block my way again!

(QUINN exits. BRAGEN slams his fist on the floor in rage and frustration.)

BRAGEN: Guard!

(*A guard enters, and goes to help him up. With an effort* BRAGEN *controls himself, and looks round the rest room.*)

The Examiner is missing. He must be found immediately.

6. *LESTERSON'S LABORATORY.*

(THE DOCTOR *is still busy examining the contents of the laboratory.* BEN *addresses* POLLY *in a loud voice.*)

BEN: Of course the *real* Doctor was always going on about the Daleks.

POLLY: The *real* Doctor?

(THE DOCTOR *looks up, and he mutters.*)

THE DOCTOR: Real Doctor? Oh... oh, you mean the *real* Doctor.

BEN: And now I've seen that claw thing... well, I wouldn't want to shake hands with it, let's put it that way.

POLLY: Doctor look, if they're that dangerous, what are you going to do about it?

THE DOCTOR: Save my breath... would Lesterson listen? Lesterson listen, Lesterson listen, Lesterson listen... exercises the tongue, try it. Lesterson listen, Lesterson listen, Lesterson listen...

BEN: Look, they think you're the Examiner... order them to destroy the Daleks... Well chuck your weight about.

POLLY: Lesterson listen, Lesterson listen, Lesterson listen, Lesterson listen, Lesterson listen, Lesterson listen, Lesterson listen...

(As POLLY *tries repeating* THE DOCTOR*'s tongue-twister to herself,* THE DOCTOR *looks up, pats* BEN *on the back, and returns to his studies. Suddenly,* POLLY *and* BEN *jump as they hear a voice outside the laboratory. The door opens and* LESTERSON *and* RESNO, *the stranger that earlier had observed* BEN *going into the capsule, enter.)*

LESTERSON: What do you think you're doing in here?

(There is no reaction from THE DOCTOR.*)*

Who gave you permission?

*(*THE DOCTOR *cuts him short by taking the examiner's badge from his lapel and thrusting it towards* LESTERSON.*)*

THE DOCTOR: Read this!

*(*LESTERSON *glances at it and goes to hand it back.)*

Aloud!

*(*LESTERSON *glares at* THE DOCTOR, *then reluctantly obeys.)*

LESTERSON: 'Accord every access...'

THE DOCTOR: Exactly! It doesn't say 'except your laboratory' any-where, does it?

*(*THE DOCTOR *takes the badge back, examines it thoroughly, and then produces a magnifying glass, with which he peers at the badge.)*

... unless it's in micro-print.

LESTERSON: I should have been asked first.

*(*THE DOCTOR *points an accusing finger at* BEN.*)*

THE DOCTOR:	What was the first thing you noticed when you looked inside that capsule?
BEN:	The, the... the Daleks.
THE DOCTOR:	You were astounded?
POLLY:	Yes.
THE DOCTOR:	Amazed?
BEN:	Yes.

(THE DOCTOR *whirls on* LESTERSON *and shouts at him.*)

THE DOCTOR: You didn't even give them a glance!

(LESTERSON *is shaken and taken off-guard, which is exactly what* THE DOCTOR *intends.*)

Why? Because you'd been in there and seen them! Where is the third Dalek?

LESTERSON: I don't know what you're talking about!

THE DOCTOR: You opened up the capsule without permission. You found the inner compartment containing three Daleks, you took one of them away and you hid it!

LESTERSON: This is... what nonsense!

(*The door to the laboratory opens and* BRAGEN *enters.* THE DOCTOR *resumes his studies at the work bench.*)

BRAGEN: May I ask what all this is about?

(*There is silence.* POLLY *is the first to crack.*)

POLLY: We opened an inner compartment in the capsule and Lesterson has already been in there...

LESTERSON: I don't deny that.

BEN: And he's nicked a Dalek.

BRAGEN: Dalek?

LESTERSON: It's the name the Examiner has given the two metal creations that I discovered inside the capsule.

BEN: Yeah, and they're dangerous... evil.

LESTERSON: Lumps of metal. Quite inactive.

BEN: That's what you think, mate... if you'd seen...

> (BEN *is interrupted by a whistle from* THE DOCTOR's *recorder.* THE DOCTOR *catches* BEN's *eye and shakes his head to silence him.*)

LESTERSON: I consider it my duty as a scientist to examine and... investigate these objects. Now please, all of you, keep out of my laboratory. Keep your hands off my experiments.

THE DOCTOR: These "lumps of metal"... Daleks... I want them broken up, or melted down. Up or down, I don't care which... but destroyed!

LESTERSON: I refuse to allow it.

> (THE DOCTOR *moves over to* BRAGEN *and brandishes his badge.*)

THE DOCTOR: I am an Earth Examiner. I demand it!

> (As BRAGEN *looks at the badge,* THE DOCTOR *gives an encouraging wink to* BEN, *as an acknowledgement of his idea to order the* DALEK *destroyed.*)

LESTERSON: You're exceeding your authority.

THE DOCTOR: Perhaps we should ask the Governor about that. I wish to see him immediately.

BRAGEN: That might be difficult.

THE DOCTOR: But not impossible. Ben... Polly?

(THE DOCTOR *moves rapidly to the door to avoid further argument.* POLLY *and* BEN *follow.* BRAGEN *glares at* LESTERSON *and then also leaves the room.*)

RESNO: Could he stop the experiments?

LESTERSON: I don't know. It's none of your business. You go and get Janley and then come back here. We haven't got any time to waste.

(RESNO *nods and moves towards the door.*)

Now go on man, quickly. Quickly!

(RESNO *hurries out.* LESTERSON *locks the door and then crosses over to the capsule. He puts a hand inside the doorway and feels around for some previously discovered opening device. There is a click, and a moment later another compartment opens. The third* DALEK *is revealed, for the moment still lifeless.*)

He won't stop me examining. There must be some way to bring you back to life... and I'm going to find it!

7. *THE REST ROOM*.

(POLLY *opens the door and enters, followed by* BEN, THE DOCTOR *and* BRAGEN.)

BRAGEN: And of course you do have the right of any access...

THE DOCTOR: Which is why I have a badge which says so.

BRAGEN: Lesterson watches over his ideas like a mother hen.

THE DOCTOR: If there was a bomb under this floor timed to go off in five minutes, would you ask my permission before you ripped up the floorboards? Aha... fruit!

> (THE DOCTOR's *analogy is somewhat shattered by this last exclamation.* THE DOCTOR *examines each piece of fruit very carefully.*)

BRAGEN: Examiner, it's up to you, of course, but I'd advise a bit of discretion in your investigations. It's not a very good time just now.

THE DOCTOR: Thank you.

BRAGEN: With all these disturbances.

POLLY: Disturbances?

BRAGEN: Yes, minor acts of sabotage... rebel cliques, secret newspapers, nothing important, you understand, but... it keeps the Governor busy... I have no doubt he'll tell you about it himself when I arrange your meeting with him.

> (THE DOCTOR *is still busy with the fruit. He picks up an apple and starts to eat it.* BEN *tries to divert attention from his odd behaviour.*)

BEN: When will that be?

BRAGEN: He's going on a tour of the perimeter of the colony. I'll... I'll find out if he can see you before he goes.

POLLY: Thank you.

> (BRAGEN *nods, gives a strained look at* THE DOCTOR, *and leaves the room.* POLLY *picks up a banana and, sitting down on the bed with* BEN, *starts to eat it.*)

BEN: You know, it's little things like this that make it difficult to believe that you're the Doctor. The other one,
I mean the proper one... oh nuts, you know what I
mean!

THE DOCTOR: Nuts, yes certainly. Here we are.... Crackers?

BEN: You, my old china... are an out and out phoney!

THE DOCTOR: China, yes, I went there once, I believe.

*(He reaches into his pocket and produces the 500-
year diary. He flicks the pages rapidly until he
finds what he is looking for.)*

Met Marco Polo!

BEN: No, not China. China! China and plate... mate...
friend!

THE DOCTOR: Yes, Marco Polo, a friend... I believe he was...

*(THE DOCTOR quickly kneels down by the bed and
starts to examine the fruit. BEN gives up in frustration.)*

POLLY: Don't listen to him, Doctor. I know who you are...

*(THE DOCTOR mimes an extravagant "Sssh' to
POLLY, holding his finger to his lips. POLLY is puzzled. THE DOCTOR produces a knife from another
pocket and carefully cuts open a piece of fruit.
Even BEN starts to watch what THE DOCTOR is
doing. THE DOCTOR pulls out from the middle of the
fruit a small microphone. He drops it on the floor
and energetically stamps on it.)*

BEN: Well, well, a touch of the bugs... microphones!

POLLY: Someone was listening to what we were saying!

BEN: Yes, so that's why you were messing about and talking nonsense!

THE DOCTOR: I never talk nonsense!

                (His face breaks into a smile as he looks at POLLY.)

                ... well, hardly never.

BEN: Well, they certainly believe in making us at home, don't they?

THE DOCTOR: At first I thought there might be more than one.

                (He grimaces, and BEN and POLLY laugh at the thought that he might have already swallowed one of the bugs.)

BEN: Here, I bet old Charlie Bragen did it.

POLLY: Charlie?

BEN: Well, 'Fred' wouldn't suit him, would it?

POLLY: If he did do it, do you think it was his own idea? I mean he could have been under orders.

BEN: From the Governor? Hmm, I don't know... what do you think, Doctor?

                (THE DOCTOR has lapsed into deep thought again. He looks up.)

THE DOCTOR: Mmm? Oh, yes... yes of course.

                (He holds up the button.)

                But let's consider the button for a moment. It's the only clue we've got to the murderer of the Examiner... The, the... *real* Examiner.

POLLY: And *who* asked for him to come?

BEN:	Well, Lesterson's crackers about that capsule. He wouldn't want anyone nosing about.
POLLY:	Bragen said the Governor's been having trouble.
BEN:	No, rule him out. Governors are all the same, he wouldn't ask for help. If he sent to Earth, it would look as though he couldn't do the job properly.
POLLY:	Yes.
BEN:	Oh, I vote we go back to the TARDIS. I've had enough of this dump.
THE DOCTOR:	Have you... what about the Daleks?
BEN:	Well... they're dead.
POLLY:	What about the thing we saw in the capsule... that was alive all right.
BEN:	Yeah, well I can't explain that.
THE DOCTOR:	I can! And that's why we have to stay!

8. LESTERSON'S LABORATORY.

(The third DALEK *is now standing in the middle of the laboratory. It is connected with a mass of wires leading from its dome to various control panels in the laboratory.* JANLEY, RESNO *and* LESTERSON *are all busy checking the wiring and fixing new ones to the* DALEK.*)*

RESNO:	Ugly-looking brutes, aren't they? What's he want to muck about with them for? Leave well alone, that's what I say.
JANLEY:	You're a fine one to be a research assistant. Leave well alone. There'll be no progress on this planet

with people like you around.

RESNO: We're doing all right as we are. Or we were until your lot came along stirring things up. You won't get away with it you know. The Governor knows all about you rebels. He'll smash the lot of you when he's ready.

JANLEY: The Governor? He couldn't smash...

LESTERSON: Will you be quiet! Where do you both think you are? This is a scientific laboratory. Kindly keep your politics out of it. Come on Resno man, get on with it. We haven't got all day. We've got to get this working before the Examiner stops us. He's got some phobia about these, these... Daleks.

9. THE REST ROOM.

(THE DOCTOR is sitting on the bed, holding his 500-year diary. POLLY and BEN are nearby.)

THE DOCTOR: I know the misery they cause... the destruction. But there's something else more terrible... something I can only half remember...

(He lapses into thought again. POLLY and BEN look at each other, impressed by the intensity of THE DOCTOR's words.)

POLLY: Doctor... what was it?

(There is a knock at the door and, as they turn, BRAGEN enters, accompanied by two guards.)

THE DOCTOR: Well? Where is the Governor? What did he say?

BRAGEN: He sends his apologies, Examiner. He can't see you tonight, but he hopes to see you first thing in the morning.

BEN: Well it might not wait that long, Char... er... Bragen.

                (He corrects himself just in time. POLLY *hides a smile.)*

BRAGEN: It will have to!

THE DOCTOR: Excuse me.

                *(*THE DOCTOR *stands up and goes to leave the room, putting on his hat as he does so.)*

BEN: Where are you going?

THE DOCTOR: To see the Governor of course.

BRAGEN: I'm afraid that's not possible. Once his door is closed, no-one, not even you, Examiner, is allowed into his room.

                *(*THE DOCTOR *seemingly acquiesces, and takes off his hat.)*

THE DOCTOR: Very well.

BRAGEN: Thank you. Until the morning, then?

                *(*BRAGEN *nods curtly and exits, followed by the guards.)*

BEN: What happens now?

THE DOCTOR: I shall radio Earth. Governor or not, Hensell will have to listen to them... I'll get Earth to back me...

                (Without warning, he leaps towards the door and yanks it open. He looks surprised that there is no-one there.)

                Funny, I could have sworn... you stay here, I shan't be long.

10. LESTERSON'S LABORATORY.

(LESTERSON *is now standing in front of a panel of electric meters, dials and switches.* RESNO *stands by a smaller bank of instruments which are connected to the* DALEK. JANLEY *is beside the* DALEK, *notebook in hand. She looks at her watch and duly makes a note of the time.*)

LESTERSON: Connecting now.

(*He pulls down several switches and a low hum fills the air. Various lights start blinking and needles start flickering.*)

RESNO: All connections responding.

(*They all look at the* DALEK. *It is still lifeless and unmoving.*)

LESTERSON: Nothing at all?

RESNO: No.

LESTERSON: Are you sure?

RESNO: There's nothing wrong here.

LESTERSON: Well let's see.

(*He goes over to inspect* RESNO's *bank of meters for himself.*)

RESNO: Really, if you can't trust me to read a dial.

LESTERSON: Be quiet. All right, we'll try again. This time we'll take it up to 3.24. Got that, Janley?

JANLEY: 3.24...

(*The humming noise rises perceptibly. They continue to watch the* DALEK. *Nothing happens at first, but then slowly its sucker-stick begins to move.)*

RESNO: It's moving!

(The DALEK's eye-stick moves very slowly into an upright position.)

LESTERSON: Now note this, Janley. Number one attachment with sucker stick responding. Number two attachment not moving. Number three attachment with lens responding. Watch these meters, Resno.

RESNO: Still responding.

(LESTERSON strolls over to the DALEK and walks around it thoughtfully.)

LESTERSON: Now it's reasonable to assume that this sucker-stick acts like some kind of a hand.

(The DALEK's sucker-stick moves outwards slightly towards JANLEY, who steps back nervously, stifling a scream.)

It's all right, don't be alarmed. We've only introduced temporary power. We'll have to open it up before we can find out how it works permanently.

JANLEY: It's a bit frightening.

LESTERSON: Yes. Now I cannot think what this short stubby arm is for.

(LESTERSON bends and examines the gun-stick.)

JANLEY: Could the lens attachment be an eye?

LESTERSON: Yes, yes, yes, yes, now... it's quite possible this er... Dalek? Now there must be some kind of directing influence, may even be a simplified brain. Positronic, I shouldn't wonder. If only we could open it up.

(The eye and sucker-sticks suddenly sag and drop lifelessly towards the floor.)

Now what?

RESNO: Everything functioning here.

LESTERSON: Yes, well perhaps the power's leaking away some-where. We'll... we'll try again.

(As the three turn to study the various dials and meters, the eye-stick of the DALEK *comes to life again, and turns to focus on* RESNO. *Some sixth sense tells* RESNO, *who whirls round just in time to see the eye-stick pointing directly at him.)*

RESNO: Look at the eye-stick!

(Immediately the DALEK'*s eye-stick drops back to point at the floor again.* LESTERSON *and* JANLEY *look at* RESNO, *and at the* DALEK, *by then a moment too late to catch the movement in the eye-stick.)*

It's watching us!

LESTERSON: Don't be absurd, Resno.

RESNO: It was, I tell you! I saw it!

LESTERSON: You can't use the phrase "watching us". You'll have us to believe the thing has intelligence next. Now get on with your work, man!

*(*LESTERSON *turns back to his machines.)*

11. THE COMMUNICATIONS ROOM.

*(*THE DOCTOR *slowly opens the door of the commu-nications room and looks around. The room is in darkness. In the centre is a large, square console*

with a transparent structure on top. THE DOCTOR *advances into the room and walks around the console. He suddenly freezes, as he sees a pair of shoes sticking out from the end of the desk. As he moves further round he sees the body of a radio mechanic, slumped unconscious on the floor. At the foot of the console* THE DOCTOR *sees three thick cables, each of which have been unevenly cut and pulled apart.* THE DOCTOR *bends down to examine the body, and then stiffens as he hears a noise, faint but unmistakable. He stand up suddenly, and tenses.)*

THE DOCTOR: I know you're there.

*(*QUINN *steps out of the shadows, holding a large pair of wire-cutters in his hand. He switches on the light.)*

QUINN: Examiner, thank goodness it's you. I have been trying to talk to you ever since you got here.

(At this point, BRAGEN *and two of his guards enter. They move quickly over to where* THE DOCTOR *and* QUINN *are standing overlooking the unconscious radio operator.)*

BRAGEN: What's happening here?

(He glares at QUINN.*)*

You again?

QUINN: What do you want?

THE DOCTOR: I found the operator unconscious.

*(*THE DOCTOR *and* BRAGEN *look from the man on the floor to the cutters in* QUINN's *hand.)*

QUINN: Yes, so did I! I was just looking at him when I heard someone moving... it must have been you.

                (QUINN looks at THE DOCTOR. BRAGEN takes the cutters from QUINN.)

BRAGEN: And these?

QUINN: I picked them up... what is all this?

THE DOCTOR: The cables have been cut.

QUINN: What!?

                (THE DOCTOR points to the severed cables. As QUINN reaches out to examine them, THE DOCTOR notices that a button is missing from QUINN's jacket, and the other buttons on his jacket exactly match the one THE DOCTOR had placed in his hand when the real EXAMINER was murdered.)

                This is serious. It's not just our own communications. We're cut off from Earth as well.

BRAGEN: The only people who'd want to do that are the rebels...

QUINN: If these muscle-boys of yours had any brains, they'd stop things like this.

                (THE DOCTOR produces the button from his pocket. He hands it to BRAGEN.)

THE DOCTOR: Bragen, I was attacked just after I landed. This is a small souvenir I collected.

                (BRAGEN looks at it. THE DOCTOR pulls QUINN's sleeve forward and BRAGEN matches it to the tear in QUINN's sleeve.)

BRAGEN: This button belongs to you, doesn't it?

QUINN: Well... yes.

BRAGEN: And you say you picked these up.

(He waves the wire-cutters.)

I suggest that you were sabotaging the communications.

QUINN: That's a lie!

BRAGEN: Having first attacked one of the engineers. I'd detain the Governor on evidence like that!

QUINN: I hope you're not thinking of detaining me, Bragen?

BRAGEN: I have no option.

(BRAGEN signals to the guards, who take hold of QUINN's arms. QUINN gives a contemptuous snort.)

I could hardly let you run around loose after this, could I? All right, guards.

QUINN: I'm warning you, Bragen.

(QUINN seems about to attack the guards, then changes his mind.)

All right, you win this time, Bragen. We'll see what it looks like in front of the Governor.

(The guards escort QUINN out of the communications room. BRAGEN turns to THE DOCTOR.)

BRAGEN: The Governor will want an enquiry. May I ask what you were doing here?

12. LESTERSON'S LABORATORY.

(LESTERSON is still working at a bank of controls, JANLEY near him. RESNO now has a small camera

on a tripod, trained on the DALEK.)

LESTERSON: Right. I've redirected power. Try working up to 4.16. Now Resno, you'll have to dodge between the camera and your meters.

RESNO: Ready.

LESTERSON: Connecting now.

(*He pulls some switches and the familiar humming noise fills the laboratory. This time it is even louder than before.* RESNO *moves to the bank of meters.*)

RESNO: All connections responding.

(*The* DALEK *moves slightly and the sucker and eye-sticks rise up once again.*)

JANLEY: It's working!

LESTERSON: Excellent. Film it now, Resno. And note the readings, Janley.

(JANLEY *starts to write down the readings, glancing rapidly at the various dials.* RESNO *moves back to the camera and adjusts it. The* DALEK's *eye-stick focuses on* RESNO. *Then the* DALEK *moves itself until its gun-stick is also trained on him.*)

It seems interested in you, Resno.

(RESNO *stands frozen with fear, staring at the* DALEK.)

What's the matter with you, man!

RESNO: I tell you it's intelligent. It's watching me, Lesterson... weighing me up. I can sense it!

LESTERSON: Don't be a fool!

RESNO: I don't like it I tell you. We don't know what these things can do.

(LESTERSON *gently, but firmly, leads* RESNO *back to the camera in front of the* DALEK.)

LESTERSON: No and we never shall do, shall we, unless we take film of every reaction. Now get on with your work, man.

(RESNO *bends down, reluctantly, to focus the camera.* LESTERSON *goes back to his post. The* DALEK'*s gun-stick suddenly fires.* RESNO *gives a short cry as he crumples to the floor.* LESTERSON *falls on the cables connecting the* DALEK *to the power source. The* DALEK *gives a jerk, and its three sticks drop lifelessly to the floor.* JANLEY *rushes over to* RESNO, *then looks back at* LESTERSON. *Her face has no trace of concern or sympathy... only calculation.*)

JANLEY: It's all right. He isn't dead.

LESTERSON: What happened?

JANLEY: Knocked out by the shock waves.

LESTERSON: We must get him to the hospital. I'll go and get help.

13. THE REST ROOM (DAY).

(THE DOCTOR *is standing by the window, playing his recorder once more.* POLLY *and* BEN *are sitting on the bed.*)

POLLY: But we've got to defend Quinn!

BEN: Yeah, I know he's innocent until he's proved guilty... but he is guilty!

POLLY: He's the Deputy Governor.

BEN: So what? I had an 'eadmaster once who got nicked for not paying his bus fare. And then there's the motive... don't forget the motive.

POLLY: Like what for instance?

BEN: Well, he's the *Deputy* Governor, right? Maybe he wants to be *Governor*.

POLLY: Oh that's ridiculous.

BEN: Well, the jacket button wasn't! And he was caught red-handed in the communications room with a pair of pliers. And don't tell me he was plucking his eyebrows neither!

POLLY: Look, there are some people you know are all right. You just know by looking at them.

(POLLY is cut short as BRAGEN knocks and immediately enters the room, without waiting.)

BRAGEN: Good morning. The enquiry is about to begin. I've been sent to escort you...

(BRAGEN moves to one side to allow the others to pass. THE DOCTOR puts an arm round each of his two companions and guides them to the door.)

14. LESTERSON'S LABORATORY.

(The DALEK, still in the centre of the laboratory, is now covered by a dark sheet. LESTERSON and JANLEY stand in the doorway. LESTERSON looks at his watch.)

LESTERSON:	Time, Janley.
JANLEY:	Time?
LESTERSON:	Yes, yes I think so. I feel quite excited.
JANLEY:	So you should, it's a wonderful achievement.
LESTERSON:	Yes, yes, but the wonderful thing, Janley, is that we don't know the full scope of this experiment. Who knows where we may go from here.

(He goes over and pulls the sheet off the DALEK. *The gun-stick is now no longer in place.)*

	Who knows what this... Dalek may do?
JANLEY:	It's harmless now?
LESTERSON:	Yes, yes, yes. I've removed it. Oh Resno, have you been to see him today?
JANLEY:	Yes, yes he's had medical attention. He's going to be all right. No-one must find out about this accident. It might give the Examiner just the excuse they want... and it could stop the whole project.
LESTERSON:	Oh, yes, yes, yes. You're right.
JANLEY:	Right... ready?
LESTERSON:	Yes. Let's go and surprise them!

*(*JANLEY *watches as* LESTERSON *folds up the sheet.)*

15. THE GOVERNOR'S TERRACE ROOM.

(The terrace is ringed with pillars. Trees and greenery abound beyond a large window. A guard is busy setting out some chairs. HENSELL *sits behind a large and impressive desk, in an equally*

large and impressive chair. He is reading some papers. BRAGEN ushers in THE DOCTOR, POLLY and BEN, and gestures to the chairs. HENSELL looks at THE DOCTOR.)

HENSELL: I'm sorry I couldn't see you earlier, Examiner. Please sit down.

(THE DOCTOR gives an ambivalent shrug and sits down alongside POLLY and BEN. HENSELL nods and the guard brings in QUINN.)

Well, Quinn. I don't like this any more than you do. What have you been up to?

QUINN: Nothing. Absolutely nothing!

(HENSELL taps the papers in front of him.)

HENSELL: Well what about Bragen's report then? These are *facts*, Quinn. Now what have you got to say about it?

QUINN: Does the engineer say I hit him?

BRAGEN: How could he if he was hit from behind?

QUINN: Then it's only circumstantial evidence.

BRAGEN: The Examiner was also attacked in the mercury swamp. We have a button from your jacket, found in the Examiner's hand.

QUINN: I can't explain that.

BRAGEN: I'm sure you can't!

(THE DOCTOR is listening intently to the proceedings. BEN is bored and stifles a couple of yawns. POLLY meanwhile is getting angrier and angrier.)

HENSELL: Examiner? You seem to be in two minds...

(BEN *mumbles to himself.*)

BEN: Yeah, and two bodies.

HENSELL: You mentioned to Bragen that these machines of Lesterson's... what do you call them?

THE DOCTOR: I call them what they are... Daleks!

HENSELL: Yes, yes, yes, Daleks. You say they could be a motive for destroying our communications?

THE DOCTOR: I do.

(LESTERSON *appears in the doorway and strides onto the terrace. He looks extremely confident and smug.*)

HENSELL: Lesterson, this is a special enquiry. Now please...

LESTERSON: I won't wait! You won't be disappointed!

(THE DOCTOR *seems to have a premonition of what is coming. He looks nervously around him.* BEN *and* POLLY *notice the look of alarm on his face.*)

HENSELL: You heard what I said, Lesterson.

LESTERSON: Governor, I've just completed an experiment which could revolutionise the whole colony. Bear with me...

(THE DOCTOR *moves towards him.*)

THE DOCTOR: Lesterson, what have you done? What have you done?

LESTERSON: I'll show you.

(*He moves to the centre of the terrace, and with a slightly mad look of triumph on his face, calls out.*)

Janley... now.

(The door slowly opens. For a moment nothing happens, then slowly a DALEK *glides in through the doorway. Everyone in the room is transfixed, half with fear, half with anticipation.* THE DOCTOR *is the only one in the room to recognise the true danger. He moves a fraction, shaking his head in despair. The* DALEK *moves around, its eye-stick seemingly searching around. It focuses on* THE DOCTOR, *who backs away in fright.* BEN *follows the angle of the* DALEK'*s eye-stick and sees the effect it is having on* THE DOCTOR.*)*

BEN: It recognised the Doctor... It recognised him!

*(*POLLY *also sees the look of terror on* THE DOC-TOR'*s face.)*

POLLY: What's the matter, Doctor? Are you all right?

*(*THE DOCTOR *shakes his head in despair.)*

THE DOCTOR: The fools... the stupid fools!

BEN: You're scared... what can it do?

THE DOCTOR: Nothing... yet!

LESTERSON: This creation is...

BEN: It knew who you were... it sounds ridiculous, but it did...

*(*THE DOCTOR *nods.)*

THE DOCTOR: It knew who I *was*.

BEN: Well if a Dalek knows who you are...

(Their conversation has gone unnoticed by the others, who are listening with rapt attention to LESTERSON.*)*

LESTERSON: ...called, I understand, a Dalek. Look at it. I have merely given it electric power. And it's capable of storing it. Moreover, it responds to orders.

(He turns to the DALEK.)

Turn around.

(The DALEK does so.)

Move that chair.

(Again the DALEK obeys.)

Stop... You see, just think what this will do to our mining programme, our processing, packaging. Dozens of labour jobs, Governor. It may even provide the end to all this colony's problems.

(THE DOCTOR moves forward and speaks to the assembled crowd, even through his eyes never leave the DALEK.)

THE DOCTOR: Yes... it will end the colony's problems... because it will end the colony!

(As though to refute this, the DALEK suddenly speaks.)

DALEK: I am your ser-vant.

(The effect on the room is immediate and dramatic.)

LESTERSON: It... it spoke! Janley, did you hear that? It can actually talk!

DALEK: I am your ser-vant.

THE DOCTOR: It can do many things, Lesterson. But the thing it does most efficiently is...

DALEK: I am your ser-vant.

THE DOCTOR: ...exterminate human beings. It destroys them...

DALEK: I am your ser-vant.

THE DOCTOR: ...without mercy, without conscience...

DALEK: I am your ser-vant.

THE DOCTOR: ...destroys them... utterly... completely. It destroys them!

> (THE DOCTOR *speaks louder and louder to compete with the* DALEK, *who is also trying to do the same thing. The* DALEK *has the louder voice.*)

DALEK: I am your ser-vant... I am your ser-vant... I am your ser-vant...

EPISODE THREE

1. THE GOVERNOR'S TERRACE ROOM (DAY).

THE DOCTOR: But the thing it does most efficiently is...

DALEK: I am your ser-vant.

THE DOCTOR: ...exterminate human beings. It destroys them...

DALEK: I am your ser-vant.

THE DOCTOR: ...without mercy, without conscience...

DALEK: I am your ser-vant.

THE DOCTOR: ...destroys them... utterly... completely. It destroys them!

> *(THE DOCTOR speaks louder and louder to compete with the DALEK, who is also trying to do the same thing. The DALEK has the louder voice.)*

DALEK: I am your ser-vant... I am your ser-vant... I am your ser-vant...

> *(QUINN moves forward, intrigued by the DALEK. The guard rests a restraining arm on his shoulder. The DALEK stops its repetitive grating and stands there, silent. THE DOCTOR stares at it, his face like*

thunder. POLLY *and* BEN *move towards him.* LESTERSON, *in the background, sneers triumphantly.* HENSELL *moves to stand beside him.*)

HENSELL: So, Lesterson... they're even capable of speech.

LESTERSON: Yes... but then why not, after all they have a certain intelligence...

HENSELL: Yes, I know, but...

LESTERSON: ...but it is an intelligence that we can control.

(BRAGEN *shoots a look at* LESTERSON, *but does not say anything.* HENSELL *returns to sit at his desk.*)

HENSELL: So what you want is permission to continue your experiments?

LESTERSON: Governor, think what it would mean if we set it to work in the mines. It could double our production overnight!

BRAGEN: Consider the effect it could have on our whole economy.

(HENSELL *gives a quick smile as he considers the possibilities.*)

HENSELL: Yes, and the effect of that on Earth. Yes... yes, they could be very grateful.

(LESTERSON *is still smirking, confident that* HENSELL *will now support him.* THE DOCTOR *is still staring at the* DALEK. *He speaks softly, but with great conviction.*)

THE DOCTOR: I shall stop you... I will!

(*The* DALEK *makes a slight move towards* THE DOCTOR. BEN *moves forward, but before anything can happen,* HENSELL *speaks.)*

HENSELL: All right Lesterson, permission granted.

THE DOCTOR: Permission? Permission for what?

LESTERSON: To continue my work, Examiner.

THE DOCTOR: But didn't you all hear what I said? The Daleks must be destroyed!

LESTERSON: Never!

THE DOCTOR: Very well, if not by my order... then by Earth's!

(He glares around, but quickly realises he has little hope of anyone listening to him.)

Come on, Ben... Polly.

(THE DOCTOR moves to the door. JANLEY is standing there. Before he leaves, however, HENSELL gets up and intercepts him.)

HENSELL: Examiner... just a moment. Tell me... why are you so against this project?

THE DOCTOR: But I've told you! I realise I can't give you any proof, but you've no idea of the danger!

LESTERSON: Oh!

(LESTERSON gives a derisive snort. THE DOCTOR whirls towards him.)

Yes... danger! I shall be contacting Earth just as soon as radio communications have been restored.

(THE DOCTOR turns and leaves the room, pausing as he does to glare again at the DALEK.)

You're my servant, are you?

DALEK: I am.

THE DOCTOR: Very well... immobilise yourself.

(At first the DALEK *ignores the order and continues to 'stare' at* THE DOCTOR.*)*

Go on. I order it... immediately!

(Suddenly the DALEK *drops its eye and sucker-sticks to the floor.* THE DOCTOR *is not fooled for a moment, and strides from the room. As soon as he is gone, the* DALEK *comes back to life again.)*

JANLEY: Lesterson!

(They both stare at the DALEK.*)*

LESTERSON: Why did you stop obeying? You were given an order.

DALEK: He has gone.

*(*LESTERSON *looks worried. This is the first sign that the* DALEK *can think for itself.)*

LESTERSON: Then you obey, only...

DALEK: His or-der was wrong. I can-not serve hu-man be-ings if I am im-mo-bil-ized. You gave me po-wer. Your or-ders are right. I serve you.

*(*LESTERSON *chuckles delightedly, but* HENSELL *is concerned.)*

HENSELL: Lesterson! Lesterson, yes it reasons... just how limit-ed is this intelligence?

LESTERSON: Now there is no cause for concern, Governor. Just you wait until you see the amount of work it can do.

*(*LESTERSON *turns back to the* DALEK.*)*

Now I'm really going to put you through your paces... Follow me, Dalek.

DALEK: I o-bey.

(LESTERSON smiles and leaves the room with JAN-LEY. The DALEK follows obediently behind them.)

2. A CORRIDOR.

(THE DOCTOR, POLLY and BEN walk down the corridor. Suddenly THE DOCTOR gives a cry, and snaps his fingers.)

THE DOCTOR: That's it!

(He digs deep into his pocket and produces a notebook and pencil. He starts to scribble down a list of requirements, screwing up his face in concentration as he writes. POLLY and BEN shake their heads.)

POLLY: We should have stayed with Quinn.

BEN: We couldn't have helped him, Polly... even if we'd wanted to. The Governor's already reached his verdict.

POLLY: But he didn't murder the real Examiner, I'm sure he didn't.

BEN: Oh, the way I see it, this lot's too busy arguing amongst themselves to do much about anything. Anyway, first things first... the Daleks are the important thing.

(THE DOCTOR pockets the book and pencil and turns to BEN.)

THE DOCTOR: Ah, congratulations Ben!

BEN: What'd I do? What'd I do?

THE DOCTOR: You just used your brain, that's what you did. The Daleks *are* the most important thing!

> (THE DOCTOR *hurries off, beckoning them to follow.* BEN *smiles, pleased at the compliment, and follows.*)

POLLY: I still think Quinn's innocent!

3. THE GOVERNOR'S TERRACE ROOM.

> (QUINN *is standing in front of* HENSELL's *desk.* HENSELL *is seated at the desk, with* BRAGEN *standing beside him.*)

QUINN: How can I be in league with the rebels?

BRAGEN: The evidence confirms it.

QUINN: It was I who warned of their dangers.

BRAGEN: As part of your overall plan.

QUINN: You wouldn't even take the matter seriously!

BRAGEN: If I was wrong then, I have a chance to rectify it now!

QUINN: If that's going to be your attitude, I...

HENSELL: Quinn! Let us conduct this enquiry in an orderly manner. Now, the Examiner was attacked, there can be no question of that.

BRAGEN: And the button grabbed by the Examiner was missing from your suit.

HENSELL: Yes, if you've got something to add to that, you'd

better say it now.

QUINN: I didn't attack the man. I had no reason to...

    (BRAGEN *makes it clear he does not believe him.*)

I was the one who sent for him!

    (HENSELL *and* BRAGEN *stare at* QUINN. HENSELL *rises from his chair.*)

HENSELL: You sent for him?

QUINN: It was necessary. Under the circumstances I'd hardly be likely to sabotage the radio communications.

HENSELL: But... but why, Quinn? Why?

QUINN: Because of the rebels!

BRAGEN: The rebels! They're nothing more than one or two fanatics...

QUINN: You know as well as I do...

BRAGEN: ...unless you're trying to create trouble here... to undermine the Governor's position?

HENSELL: Bragen... you'd better explain that.

BRAGEN: If you are removed, who takes your place? The Deputy Governor of course. And that's the real reason behind all this trouble, isn't it Quinn?

HENSELL: Go on.

BRAGEN: You attack the Examiner in the mercury swamp and blame it on the rebels, then you sabotage the radio... blame that on the rebels too.

    (HENSELL *looks from* QUINN *to* BRAGEN, *and makes his decision.*)

HENSELL: Get him out of my sight.

                (BRAGEN *smiles triumphantly at* QUINN, *then turns to the guard, who starts to march* QUINN *out of the room.*)

QUINN: Hensell, before you listen to these preposterous allegations...

                (HENSELL *sits down at his desk, saddened by what has happened.*)

HENSELL: I chose Quinn myself. I trained him for the job... Why, in a few years' time he would have had this seat.

BRAGEN: Sometimes, Governor, a few years is a long time to wait.

                (HENSELL *nods, then waves his hand to dismiss* BRAGEN. BRAGEN *looks as though he's not going to be dismissed so easily, then changes his mind and starts to leave.*)

HENSELL: Oh, Bragen?

BRAGEN: Governor?

HENSELL: You will assume Quinn's duties. As of now, you are Deputy Governor.

                (As BRAGEN *leaves, he smiles to himself, having successfully achieved his purpose.*)

                4. THE REST ROOM.

                (THE DOCTOR *is holding a chair above his head. He crashes it down, onto a piece of electrical equipment, which shatters under the impact, spilling its innards all over the floor.* THE DOCTOR *chortles with childlike glee.* BEN *and* POLLY *watch in amazement.)*

THE DOCTOR: Ah!

BEN: I hope you know what you're doing!

THE DOCTOR: So do I!

(He puts the chair down and bends over to examine the various transistors, etc, that are on the floor. He produces his magnifying glass for a closer examination.)

Excellent. Excellent!

BEN: But I thought we were after the Daleks... not this control unit you've nicked.

*(*THE DOCTOR *is not paying attention. He moves around the room, searching for something.)*

THE DOCTOR: If only we could find a... ah, yes!

(He sees the bed, scurries across to it, and starts pulling off the pillows and sheets. When he is down to the bare frame, he pulls off one of the metal struts that span the frame. The other end of the strut is more securely fastened and does not come away so easily.)

BEN: He's a right little delinquent, in 'e?

POLLY: Doctor. What on Earth are you up to?

*(*THE DOCTOR *is jerking the strut up and down, trying to make it snap. Finally it gives, and he falls backwards with a yelp of glee at his success.)*

THE DOCTOR: Now we're really getting somewhere!

BEN: Look Doctor, I don't want to appear dim, but how's this going to do the Daleks in?

THE DOCTOR: They think that Lesterson's the driving force, but I don't. The Daleks are using him!

POLLY: But how?

THE DOCTOR: Problem: smash the Daleks and the people here will lock us up or kill us. Let the Daleks go and we'll all be exterminated.

BEN: We could just go back to the TARDIS... at least we'd be safe to think there.

THE DOCTOR: Yes... Getting on...

                (THE DOCTOR returns his attention to the shattered control unit, taking the piece of metal with him. He sits down on the floor and starts to build something.)

BEN: Talk to him, will you?

POLLY: Doctor look, if you told us what you were up to, perhaps we could help you.

THE DOCTOR: Mustn't underestimate any of them. Lesterson's a first class scientist... first class. He opened the capsule; he realised that the Daleks could be reactivated.

BEN: Yeah, that could be the answer. Let's kidnap Lesterson, and hide him away for a bit...

                (POLLY looks at BEN with a look of scorn on her face.)

                Well, it'd stop him bringing the Daleks back to life, wouldn't it?

                (POLLY turns back to THE DOCTOR, showing how

much she thinks of BEN's *idea.* BEN *mutters to himself.)*

I thought it was pretty bright...

THE DOCTOR: There we are.

(He makes some final adjustments, pockets his tools, looks at the leftover pieces of electrical debris and pockets those too. POLLY *looks at the device* THE DOCTOR *has constructed, but it is completely unfamiliar to her.* BEN *looks at it too.)*

BEN: What is it?

THE DOCTOR: What is it? It could be the answer to all our problems.

5. *A CORRIDOR.*

*(*QUINN *is being marched along by an armed guard. They reach the end of the corridor, just as* THE DOCTOR, POLLY *and* BEN *appear, on their way to the laboratory.* QUINN *pauses, glad of the chance to appeal directly to* THE EXAMINER.*)*

QUINN: Ah Examiner, don't let them fool you about the rebels. They're strong...

(The guard tries to move QUINN *on, but he resists.)*

Try and find out where they hold their meetings.

(The guard tries to push QUINN *away.)*

POLLY: Leave him alone!

QUINN: It's all right, Polly.

*(*QUINN *is hustled away by the guard.* POLLY *goes to follow, but* THE DOCTOR *gently restrains her.)*

THE DOCTOR: We'll help him, Polly, but... later.

                (POLLY *isn't convinced, and looks after* QUINN.)

POLLY: Yes, but...

THE DOCTOR: This is a case where a little injustice is better than wholesale slaughter. What we want is in Lesterson's laboratory. Come along.

                6. LESTERSON'S LABORATORY.

                (LESTERSON *is sitting on a chair with a stopwatch in his hand, directly in front of the* DALEK. JANLEY *stands with a notepad in her hand.*)

LESTERSON: Incredible! Let's move on to test fourteen.

DALEK: I am rea-dy.

LESTERSON: When sodium acts on ethyl alcohol, what is the resulting derivative?

DALEK: Sod-i-um eth-ox-ide. C - 2 - H - 5 - O - N - A.

                (JANLEY *writes and checks this on the notepad.*)

LESTERSON: Just five seconds, Janley! Just the time it took to speak the answer.

JANLEY: Right, too.

LESTERSON: Yes, of course it's right. Can you imagine what kind of positronic brain this robot has, Janley? Think of the store of knowledge that it must carry.

                (*He turns back to the* DALEK.)

    Sulphuric acid?

DALEK: H - 2 - S - O - 4.

LESTERSON: Ah, you see?

(The laboratory door opens and THE DOCTOR *enters, followed by* POLLY *and* BEN. THE DOCTOR *beams at* LESTERSON, *with exaggerated friendliness.)*

THE DOCTOR: May I come in?

LESTERSON: What do you want?

THE DOCTOR: Oh, just to see how you're getting on.

LESTERSON: If you think...

*(*THE DOCTOR *is sweetness and light, and behaving as if newly admitted to the* LESTERSON *fan club.)*

THE DOCTOR: No, please. I'm not here to cause trouble. I'm just interested, that's all.

LESTERSON: You've done nothing but meddle and interfere ever since you landed on Vulcan.

THE DOCTOR: Well, I... I did give you permission to open up the capsule, didn't I? Please, carry on.

*(*LESTERSON *still regards* THE DOCTOR *with some suspicion.)*

LESTERSON: And you won't try to stop me?

THE DOCTOR: Stop you? No, of course not. We got off on the wrong foot, Lesterson, but... but I'm a reasonable man, and I've been thinking. Perhaps I was hasty...

LESTERSON: Well, if you... if you really want to call a truce...

THE DOCTOR: A truce? My dear fellow, I... I'd like to be friends.

LESTERSON: Yes, yes. Very well, you may stay.

THE DOCTOR: Oh thank you. Thank you.

(He beams even more, but as LESTERSON *turns back,* THE DOCTOR *grimaces at* POLLY *and* BEN *and whispers to them.)*

Perhaps you two could amuse yourselves for a little while.

*(*THE DOCTOR *hustles them towards the door, quickly, before* LESTERSON *changes his mind. As he does there is a buzz from a console.* JANLEY *goes over and picks up a receiver.* LESTERSON *gathers up his papers and starts to show* THE DOCTOR *his results.)*

JANLEY: Laboratory.

*(*JANLEY *listens, then glances back behind herself and continues in a lower voice.)*

Yes... all right, I can come now. Bye.

(She replaces the receiver and surreptitiously picks up a cloth-covered bundle from a nearby bench. She starts to leave the laboratory.)

I've just have to slip out for a few minutes, Lesterson. All right?

LESTERSON: Yes, yes, very well then. Examiner, shall we...

(He does not look up from his papers. JANLEY *exits.)*

...test its knowledge of physics?

THE DOCTOR: Oh splendid, splendid... Please, please carry on.

LESTERSON: Thank you. What is the first law of thermodynamics?

DALEK: When heat is trans-formed in-to a-ny oth-er kind of en-er-gy or vice ver-sa the to-tal quan-ti-ty of en-er-gy re-mains in-var-i-ab-le. That is to say the quan-ti-ty of heat which dis-ap-pears...

(As LESTERSON *is listening to the* DALEK, *his back to* THE DOCTOR, THE DOCTOR *produces his device from a pocket and fixes it to an instrument panel. As he is doing this, the* DALEK *turns and looks at what he is doing, sensing that something is wrong.* THE DOCTOR *flicks a switch on the device and there is a terrible mechanical screeching. The* DALEK *starts to whirl around, out of control, its eye-stick and sucker-sticks jerking violently, its voice rapidly rising in pitch.)*

...is e-quiv-al-ent to the quan-ti-ty of the oth-er kind of en-er-gy pro-duced and vice ver-sa.

*(*LESTERSON *sees what* THE DOCTOR *has done and rushes over. He pushes* THE DOCTOR *aside, and picking up the device, hurls it to the floor.)*

LESTERSON: You fool! What do you think you're doing?

THE DOCTOR: I'm saving your life.

LESTERSON: Get out. Get out!

(The DALEK *is slowly recovering.)*

DALEK: I have sus-tained no dam-age.

7. *THE GOVERNOR'S TERRACE ROOM.*

JANLEY: It's all right, it's me.

(She enters, carrying the bundle she took from the laboratory. BRAGEN *is standing near the desk and is clearly expecting her.)*

BRAGEN: You were able to get away then?

JANLEY: Yes, Lesterson's with the Examiner. And Hensell?

BRAGEN: At a meeting of production managers. He left me in control.

JANLEY: We could take over the colony now.

BRAGEN: No. No, it has to be absolutely right. I don't want to take over a colony full of rebels, do I Janley?

JANLEY: I don't know. You're making me help them.

BRAGEN: Only to stir them up to create enough trouble to get rid of Hensell. And then...

              (BRAGEN *sits down and puts his feet up on the desk.*)

              ...then we crush them. The whole colony will be grateful... and I'll be Governor.

              (JANLEY *unwraps the bundle. Inside is the* DALEK'*s gun-stick.*)

              Is that the gun you told me of?

JANLEY: U'ha.

BRAGEN: Can you persuade the rebels this will help them?

JANLEY: Yes. Valmar thinks he can work in a switch to turn it on and off.

BRAGEN: How powerful is it?

JANLEY: It killed Resno, Lesterson's assistant. Lesterson believes that Resno's simply shaken up... taking a few days off.

BRAGEN: And the body?

JANLEY: In the mercury swamp. Lesterson was the indirect cause of Resno's death. It's a good hold over him if he makes trouble.

(BRAGEN *looks at* JANLEY, *surprised by her callousness.*)

I'll give this to Valmar then?

BRAGEN: Yes.

JANLEY: When do we move?

BRAGEN: I need another card in my hand. The Examiner bothers me...

JANLEY: I thought Quinn was the danger.

BRAGEN: Not any more... and the Examiner's no fool. No... there has to be something else.

(BRAGEN *thinks for a moment, then suddenly smiles. He has an idea.*)

8. A CORRIDOR.

(POLLY *is standing in the corridor, looking up and down.* BEN *appears and goes up to* POLLY.)

POLLY: Well?

BEN: Well, he's not in the laboratory... Lesterson's by himself.

POLLY: Hmm. He must have gone another way. Can I leave it to you? I'm going to go back to the rest room.

BEN: Well, but...

POLLY: Somebody's got to clear it up.

BEN: Okay.

(BEN walks off. POLLY goes in the opposite direction. JANLEY has been watching them, and as soon as POLLY is alone she moves to intercept her.)

JANLEY: Hello there.

(POLLY looks blank for a moment, then she remembers where she has seen JANLEY before.)

POLLY: Hello. You're Lesterson's assistant, aren't you?

JANLEY: Yes. You're not looking for the Examiner are you?

POLLY: Do you know where he is?

JANLEY: Yes, he's waiting to get a message through to Earth. He's in the communications room.

(POLLY looks none the wiser.)

POLLY: Er...?

JANLEY: You'll find it easily enough, it's around, then to the right... in the next block.

POLLY: Thanks very much.

JANLEY: 'bye.

(POLLY smiles, and goes off in the direction indicated. JANLEY watches her go and, smiling to herself, starts to follow POLLY.)

9. THE COMMUNICATIONS ROOM.

(POLLY opens the door of the room, which is in complete darkness.)

POLLY: Doctor? Anyone here?

(She moves forward into the room with growing apprehension. VALMAR *grabs her from behind and puts his hand around her mouth to prevent her from screaming.* POLLY *struggles in vain.* JANLEY *comes into the room. She takes a small ampoule from her pocket and a handkerchief. She breaks the ampoule into the handkerchief and holds it to* POLLY's *mouth.* POLLY *struggles for a few moments more and then loses consciousness.* VALMAR *lowers her to the ground as* JANLEY *switches on the light.)*

JANLEY: Well done, Valmar. There... that'll keep her quiet for a bit.

VALMAR: I've got no idea who she is... she was just snooping around.

JANLEY: I sent her. We want her kept out of the way. Get a couple of your men to keep her in a safe place.

*(*VALMAR *nods.* JANLEY *shows the* DALEK *gun to him.)*

Now this is what I told you about.

*(*VALMAR *takes the gun and examines it.)*

VALMAR: Yes... the lethal power must come from here... it should have quite a good range.

JANLEY: Can you fix it?

VALMAR: Easy. This could win us the revolution.

10. THE REST ROOM.

*(*THE DOCTOR *is again seated on the bed, playing his recorder.* BEN *is pacing up and down.)*

BEN:	She said she was coming back here. She knew the way, and she wouldn't have wandered off, I know she wouldn't. Oh!

(THE DOCTOR *continues playing.* BEN *looks at him and, realising that he will not get an answer, goes over and shakes* THE DOCTOR's *shoulder.* THE DOCTOR *stops playing and looks up at* BEN.)

THE DOCTOR:	Ben, if you were a Dalek, what would be your next move?
BEN:	I'm talking about Polly.
THE DOCTOR:	Oh no, no, no, no. She's a clever girl, but she couldn't answer this...
BEN:	But she is missing!
THE DOCTOR:	Oh no, no, no.
BEN:	Oh, yes, yes, yes, yes!
THE DOCTOR:	No, no, no. She's looking around. There's a lot to see here in the colony... she's interested. I like that.

(BEN *suddenly makes a decision, and grabbing* THE DOCTOR *by the arm, starts to drag him off the bed.*)

BEN:	Come on.
THE DOCTOR:	Where are we going?
BEN:	To report it. If we make a fool of ourselves, I don't care. We report it!

(BEN *leads and half drags* THE DOCTOR *out of the room.*)

11. LESTERSON'S LABORATORY.

(LESTERSON is checking over the DALEK's external casing.)

LESTERSON: Yes... yes, yes. I managed to stop that fool of an Examiner just in time. You know there are some people here who believe that you're an enemy.

DALEK: I am your ser-vant.

(The DALEK swivels around and looks at a piece of machinery.)

What does this mach-ine do?

LESTERSON: You know, it's amazing. You have an almost human interest, and curiosity.

DALEK: A Da-lek is bet... is not the same as a hu-man. If I am to help I must know ev-er-y-thing.

LESTERSON: Yes... yes, of course.

DALEK: What is this mach-ine?

LESTERSON: It computes meteorite storms as they approach our weather satellites.

DALEK: How acc-ur-ate is it?

LESTERSON: About seventy percent. It helps to cut down on our satellite loss.

DALEK: Da-leks can build com-put-ers with one hun-dred per cent acc-ur-acy.

LESTERSON: One hundred percent?

DALEK: If you pro-vide mat-er-i-als and our own po-wer u-nit, a com-put-er will be built.

LESTERSON: A hundred percent! That would be an enormous saving for the colony.

DALEK: Then you will get the mat-er-i-als.

LESTERSON: I'll go and speak to the Governor at once.

DALEK: I will be rea-dy to dic-tate the blue print when you return.

> (LESTERSON *looks at the* DALEK *for a moment in awe, and then turns to go. The* DALEK *watches him go. As soon as it is alone, the* DALEK *glides over to the door and listens. Once it is sure that* LESTERSON *is not coming back, it goes over to the power unit, where it extends its sucker-stick and alters the controls. The hum from the unit changes in pitch. The* DALEK *turns and goes over to the capsule and enters.)*

> *12. A CORRIDOR.*

> (BEN *walks down the corridor. He glances back and realises that* THE DOCTOR *is not in sight. A few seconds later* THE DOCTOR *comes into view, busily calculating something on his fingers, his face screwed up in concentration.)*

BEN: You agreed we'd go and see Bragen.

THE DOCTOR: Hmm? Power... we know that.

BEN: Well, come on then.

THE DOCTOR: Now the energy intake of the Daleks should be the cubed...

> *(He realises that he will not manage this calculation in his head. He pulls out a pencil, and then looks*

around for something to write on. He sees a notice board nearby, and rips a notice from it, on which he starts to scribble furiously. A few moments later he shakes his head and screws up the paper.)

BEN: Now what are you up to?

THE DOCTOR: Two to the power...

BEN: Talk to yourself.

THE DOCTOR: Oh, it's useless with incomplete data!

(He is about to throw the screwed up paper on the floor, then remembers where he got it from. With a guilty look, he tries to smooth out the paper and pins it back on the board. A passer-by stares, and THE DOCTOR *smiles innocently.* LESTERSON *suddenly comes out into the corridor.* THE DOCTOR *sees him and instantly tries to hide himself and* BEN.*)*

                Lesterson!

BEN: Eh?

THE DOCTOR: He just went past... that means we can get into his laboratory again.

BEN: But we...

THE DOCTOR: Come on, come on.

(They hurry along to the laboratory, THE DOCTOR *practically running.)*

13. LESTERSON'S LABORATORY.

(As they enter they can see that the room is empty and that the door to the capsule is open.)

BEN: There's somebody in there.

> (THE DOCTOR *and* BEN *go over to the capsule. Suddenly a* DALEK *glides out from the capsule, barring their way.*)

DALEK: What are you do-ing here?

THE DOCTOR: Stand aside. Servants shouldn't question.

DALEK: En-try is re-strict-ed.

THE DOCTOR: Not for me it isn't. 'Accord every access'. I've got a badge.

DALEK: That is an or-der.

THE DOCTOR: A Dalek order. Short circuit the generator, Ben.

> (BEN *moves towards the power generator, but the* DALEK *moves to intercept him.*)

DALEK: Aaagh! Aaagh! Stand back!

THE DOCTOR: Don't be frightened Ben, it's not armed. I'm going to see what it was doing in there.

> (THE DOCTOR *darts towards the capsule. As he reaches the door two more* DALEKS *move from within to block the door. Both of them have their gun-sticks in place.* THE DOCTOR's *eyes widen as he realises with horror what this means. He whispers to* BEN.)

Ben... let's get out of here.

BEN: That fool Lesterson must have re-activated 'em.

> (THE DOCTOR *starts to back away.* BEN *nods and edges towards the laboratory door.*)

THE DOCTOR: Yes, when I say 'run', run like a rabbit... Run!

(The DALEKS *do not attempt to stop them, and they run out of the door.)*

FIRST DALEK: I have sent the hu-man be-ing for mat-er-i-als.

SECOND DALEK: And po-wer?

FIRST DALEK: Yes. Po-wer we can turn in-to sta-tic. Then we will con-quer.

(All three DALEKS *chorus in unison.)*

DALEKS: We will con-quer. We will con-quer. We will con-quer!

14. THE GOVERNOR'S TERRACE ROOM.

*(*THE DOCTOR *and* BEN *are arguing with* BRAGEN, HENSELL *and* LESTERSON.*)*

THE DOCTOR: But if you didn't do it Lesterson, then the Dalek must have used your power supply and reactivated the others itself.

LESTERSON: I was going to do that anyway.

BEN: Are you off your 'ead, mate? Those two are armed!

LESTERSON: Then we turn off the electricity, disarm them... and then everything is safe again.

(He speaks slowly, as if to a naive child, unaware that it is he who is being naive.)

THE DOCTOR: I've already explained to you...

HENSELL: Stop these arguments, both of you. I've had enough.

(He looks at THE DOCTOR.*)*

I've every confidence in Lesterson. He has carte

	blanche with the Daleks from now on.
THE DOCTOR:	But they must be destroyed!
HENSELL:	Bragen. I'm making a tour of the perimeter. I've put you in direct charge here. See that Lesterson has everything he wants, will you?

(HENSELL turns abruptly and leaves the room. LESTERSON looks pointedly at THE DOCTOR.)

LESTERSON:	I shall need a permanent guard on my laboratory, Bragen.

(THE DOCTOR stalks out of the room, followed by BEN.)

Don't worry about the Examiner... I think I can keep him quiet.

15. THE REST ROOM.

(The door bursts open and THE DOCTOR and BEN walk in.)

BEN:	We've been forgetting about Polly.
THE DOCTOR:	Greed and ambition, that's all it is. Wait 'til they find out what their precious production figures have cost them!

(There is a knock at the door. BEN opens the door and BRAGEN enters. THE DOCTOR snorts in disgust, sits down on a chair with his back to BRAGEN and starts to play his recorder.)

BEN:	Ah, I want to see you.
BRAGEN:	What about?

BEN: It's Polly... she's missing... we can't find her any-
                  where.

BRAGEN: I'll tell one of my men to make enquiries. It shouldn't
                  take long to find her.

BEN: Thanks.

                  *(BRAGEN goes over to talk to THE DOCTOR, who
                  shuffles his chair round so that he still has his
                  back towards him.)*

BRAGEN: Examiner, some of my men have found a body in the
                  mercury swamp.

                  *(For a moment THE DOCTOR stops playing his
                  recorder in shock. Then, as if to cover up his con-
                  cern he carries on again.)*

                  It was the body of a middle-aged man.

                  *(BRAGEN waits. THE DOCTOR takes the recorder
                  from his mouth.)*

THE DOCTOR: What has that to do with me?

BRAGEN: You're the Examiner... or maybe you're not.

                  (THE DOCTOR stands up and faces BRAGEN.)

THE DOCTOR: Just exactly what do you mean by that?

BRAGEN: Who are you? Quinn's friends? Come to stir up
                  rebellion?

THE DOCTOR: There's only one possible way that you could know
                  that I'm not the Examiner...

BEN: Yeah, by knowing what the real Examiner looked
                  like!

THE DOCTOR: Exactly, Ben... exactly! Only two people knew of his arrival on this planet. Myself... and his murderer!

BRAGEN: That's enough!

BEN: Is it? Doctor, we've got to tell the Governor.

BRAGEN: Do you think he'll believe you? I'll soon convince him that you murdered the man yourself... You stole the Examiner's badge.

THE DOCTOR: Then why don't you arrest us? Because there's a doubt, isn't there? Because it might, it just might, go against you.

BRAGEN: All right, all right. So neither of us wants to make a move. But you leave Lesterson alone... and the Daleks.

(He turns and stalks out.)

BEN: He'd make a right Father Christmas, wouldn't he?

THE DOCTOR: Oh, I'd rather fight a hundred of his sort, than just one Dalek.

(A movement catches BEN's eye as an envelope is pushed under the door. He hurries over to the door and flings it open, but there is no-one in sight. He picks up the envelope and opens it.)

BEN: Listen to this... 'The girl is safe. She will remain so as long as you leave the Daleks alone...'

16. LESTERSON'S LABORATORY.

(LESTERSON is standing beside the work bench, holding a DALEK gun-stick. A DALEK stands beside him.)

LESTERSON: And did you disarm the other two?

DALEK: Yes. We are your ser-vants. We do not need guns.

LESTERSON: I'm very glad. I knew the Examiner was wrong about
                     you.

DALEK: Did you get our mat-er-i-als?

LESTERSON: Yes. Everything you need you can have.

DALEK: And a po-wer plant?

LESTERSON: Everything.

                     (As he turns away, two DALEKS *glide out of the
                     capsule.)*

FIRST DALEK: We will get our po-wer.

                     (The other two DALEKS *join in the chorus.)*

SECOND & THIRD   We will get our po-wer. We will get our po-wer. We
DALEKS: will get our po-wer. We will get our po-wer. We will
                     get our po-wer...

EPISODE FOUR

1. LESTERSON'S LABORATORY (DAY).

DALEK: Did you get our mat-er-i-als?

LESTERSON: Yes. Everything you need you can have.

DALEK: And a po-wer plant?

LESTERSON: Everything.

(As he turns away, two DALEKS glide out of the capsule.)

FIRST DALEK: We will get our po-wer.

(The other two DALEKS join in the chorus.)

SECOND AND
THIRD DALEKS: We will get our po-wer. We will get our po-wer. We will get our po-wer. We will get our po-wer. We will get our po-wer...

(The three DALEKS continue this chant. LESTERSON frowns slightly, disturbed by their single-mindedness. For a moment a shadow of doubt crosses his mind. He nods thoughtfully and strolls casually over to the power generator. He switches the supply down from full to half power. Immediately, the

DALEKS' *eye and sucker-sticks droop and their voices start to run down.)*

FIRST DALEK: Turn... back... the... po-wer... sup-ply.

LESTERSON: I will, I will. But I want you to remember that I control you.

FIRST DALEK: We... are... your...ser-vants.

LESTERSON: I know. Remember it. I gave you each a special charge to bring you back to life. Any further power you need must come from this generator.

(He moves over to the DALEKS.)

And I control it. Is that clear?

FIRST DALEK: We... o-bey.

(He moves back to the generator and turns the power up to full. Two of the DALEKS *go back into the capsule. The other one stays outside.)*

LESTERSON: Where are they going?

DALEK: To a-wait your or-ders, mas-ter.

LESTERSON: Good. Have you completed the blueprints for the meteor storm computer?

DALEK: It is rea-dy.

(The DALEK *moves to the work bench.* LESTERSON *sees several thin sheets of metal and starts to examine them, fascinated.)*

LESTERSON: Oh... it's marvellous.

(He smiles at the DALEK.)

I'm glad we understand each other.

DALEK: We un-der-stand the hu-man mind.

                  2. THE GOVERNOR'S TERRACE ROOM.

                  (BRAGEN is seated at the desk, working on some papers. He is wearing a smart, new-looking uniform. VALMAR, who is an engineer, is working on a cable leading to a communications set to the left of the desk.)

BRAGEN: Isn't that finished yet?

VALMAR: Nearly.

                  (VALMAR picks up the receiver on the device.)

                  This is Valmar... Hensell please.

                  (He replaces the receiver. Almost immediately the device rings and he picks up the receiver again.)

                  Terrace. I can hear you clearly all right, good. I'm trying to get in connection now with the interior, and then the perimeter stations.

                  (VALMAR hangs up the receiver and turns to BRAGEN, who is now standing looking down at him.)

                  Well, no troubles now.

BRAGEN: Well about time. This work should have been completed long before this.

VALMAR: I did the best I could.

BRAGEN: Well it isn't good enough!

VALMAR: Then get someone else, Bragen.

BRAGEN: Be careful!

> *(VALMAR and* BRAGEN *glare at each other. Eventually* VALMAR *turns away.* BRAGEN *smiles.)*

Remember, I shall be watching you, Valmar, after this... now get out!

> *(VALMAR obeys.* BRAGEN *goes back to sit at his desk. From outside there is the sound of angry voices, then* THE DOCTOR *and* BEN *burst in, quickly followed by a* GUARD.)*

What does this intrusion mean?

GUARD: I'm sorry, Bragen. I tried to stop them.

THE DOCTOR: Intrusion? There's no intrusion. We're just returning the various calls you made. This guard tried to tell us you were busy. You're not a bit, are you?

> *(BRAGEN signals to the* GUARD *to leave.)*

BRAGEN: All right... I'll see him.

> *(The* GUARD *salutes and exits. As* THE DOCTOR *passes* BRAGEN *he notices his uniform.)*

THE DOCTOR: Oh, what a nice new uniform. Very smart, very smart. I would like a hat like that.

BRAGEN: Well, what do you want?

BEN: Some joker has kidnapped Polly and sent us this note.

THE DOCTOR: Yes.

BEN: Well, we want to know what you're doing to find her.

BRAGEN: Now that the communications are restored we can start a search.

BEN: Yeah, I can just imagine what kind of job you'll make of that. Haven't you heard anything yet?

BRAGEN: The planet is a large one...

(As he speaks a DALEK *enters the room, holding with its sucker-stick a tray, on which is a drink.* THE DOCTOR *picks up a chair and holds it in front of him, as if to keep the* DALEK *at bay.)*

THE DOCTOR: So! They've given you the run of the colony, have they?

DALEK: We o-bey.

(The DALEK *moves across to* BRAGEN *who takes the glass.)*

Do I bring li-quid for your vi-sit-ors?

BRAGEN: No. They won't be staying much longer.

(The DALEK *moves away and* THE DOCTOR *puts down the chair.)*

BEN: Look, Doctor, if he's not going to help us we'll have to search for Polly ourselves.

BRAGEN: Sound advice. Why don't you, Doctor?

THE DOCTOR: Ah, ah... Examiner.

(As they turn to leave, THE DOCTOR *whispers to* BEN.*)*

I wonder how much longer they'll be able to move around on these floors?

BEN: Eh?

THE DOCTOR: Floors. They're not metal.

BEN:	Doctor?

(As they leave the terrace, there is a buzz from a scanner on the desk. BRAGEN flicks a switch and HENSELL appears on the screen.)

HENSELL:	Ah, there you are Bragen. Thank heavens the communications are working again. It's bad enough being stuck out here on the perimeter. Well? Your report man. Hurry up. I've a very full schedule.
BRAGEN:	There *is* nothing to report, Governor.
HENSELL:	The Examiner?
BRAGEN:	I'm taking good care of him.
HENSELL:	Good, you know my orders.
BRAGEN:	Yes, sir.
HENSELL:	All right, well you can reach me here if you have to... that's all.
BRAGEN:	One moment, Governor... when will you be coming back?
HENSELL:	Oh, not for a day or two at least. You can manage, can't you?
BRAGEN:	Yes, yes of course, Governor.

(HENSELL nods and his picture fades from view. BRAGEN smiles, turns around and finds a DALEK standing in front of the desk. He is startled.)

What do you want?

(The DALEK is silent for a moment, as if weighing BRAGEN up.)

DALEK:	Have you fin-ished your li-quid?

BRAGEN: No. No I haven't!

               (The DALEK *moves backwards slightly, and then silently moves away.* BRAGEN *stares after it, suddenly afraid.)*

               3. A CORRIDOR.

               *(*JANLEY *pins up a notice on the notice board. She looks warily up and down the corridor, then walks quickly away. A man named* KEBBLE *appears at the far end of the corridor, and as* JANLEY *reaches him, she stops him, and nods back to the notice board.)*

JANLEY: You'd better check the agenda.

KEBBLE: I'll do it now.

               *(*KEBBLE *goes over to the board, unaware that* THE DOCTOR *and* BEN *are coming down the corridor towards him.* THE DOCTOR *is fiddling with a large magnet.)*

THE DOCTOR: Static. You see they need a constant supply of static from the floor, some sort of... electrical field.

BEN: Doctor!

               *(*THE DOCTOR *stares as* KEBBLE *moves away from the board. His eyes narrow.)*

               Why should he...

               *(*THE DOCTOR *and* BEN *are interrupted as three* DALEKS *glide past them down the corridor.)*

THE DOCTOR: It's madness!

BEN: Eh?

THE DOCTOR: Letting them run around like this.

BEN: Hey, wait a minute! Bragen had one acting as servant... and we've just left him!

THE DOCTOR: One Dalek in Bragen's office... three Daleks just gone down the corridor. That makes four!

BEN: Where did the fourth one come from?

THE DOCTOR: Well, Lesterson can't be making them... perhaps there were more in the capsule than we thought?

BEN: We must go and see Lesterson. Yeah, show him this note. Maybe he or Janley knows where Polly is.

(THE DOCTOR *goes over to the notice board and starts to read the various notices. He sees nothing of interest and they move off. As soon as they are gone,* KEBBLE *reappears, takes out a notebook and carefully writes something down from the board.* THE DOCTOR *and* BEN *suddenly reappear, and* KEBBLE *instantly hides the notebook and moves away.)*

We frightened him off!

(THE DOCTOR *again examines the board.)*

I wonder what the fascination of this notice board is?

THE DOCTOR: It looks like a perfectly ordinary notice board to me.

BEN: Yeah, well come on, Doctor. We must find out who's got Polly.

(THE DOCTOR *nods thoughtfully, and glances one more time at the board.* BEN *calls back impatiently from down the corridor.)*

Doctor, come on!

(THE DOCTOR follows BEN. A moment later KEBBLE reappears and continues to copy something from the board.)

4. LESTERSON'S LABORATORY.

(LESTERSON walks into the laboratory. JANLEY, sat on a stool near the instrument panels, seems surprised to see him.)

LESTERSON: Janley?

JANLEY: What is it?

LESTERSON: The Daleks. They've given me another list of materials they need.

JANLEY: Let me see.

          (LESTERSON hands her the list.)

          We've got all these things?

LESTERSON: Yes, but why these quantities, Janley? Why? How can they have used up all the materials I gave them, what is it... why, it's only a matter of a few hours ago...

JANLEY: They're building new things for us.

LESTERSON: Yes, but I don't want them to do anything without consulting me. What is it they do inside there?

          (He turns and looks into the gloomy interior of the capsule.)

JANLEY: You worry too much.

LESTERSON: Look Janley, say what you like, but I'm beginning to believe that the Examiner is right about the Daleks.

	Their original thinking terrifies me. If we can control them, fine. But if not...
JANLEY:	Yes?
LESTERSON:	Then I shall have them destroyed. It's too dangerous. The Examiner knows something about them that we don't. I'm going to ask his advice.
JANLEY:	I wouldn't bring the Examiner into it if I were you.
LESTERSON:	Why not?
JANLEY:	You want him to find out about Resno?
LESTERSON:	A little accident. How is he? Is he better?
JANLEY:	He's dead.
LESTERSON:	What are you talking about. You told me he was...
JANLEY:	You were busy with the experiments on the Daleks.
LESTERSON:	But you should have told me. The body... it'll have to be reported...
JANLEY:	Don't worry, no-one will find the body.
LESTERSON:	Oh Janley, you've done a terrible thing.
JANLEY:	The experiments on the Daleks were more important.
LESTERSON:	More important than human life? No... no, I won't accept that.
JANLEY:	You will... you must! Your carelessness was the cause of Resno's death. You know it. It's only your word against mine.
LESTERSON:	I won't be blackmailed by you!
JANLEY:	All I want is for you to go on as you are. Scientific discovery can't stop dead, Lesterson.

> *(As* JANLEY *speaks,* THE DOCTOR *and* BEN *enter the laboratory.)*

LESTERSON: I told the guards that no-one was to be allowed in.

THE DOCTOR: 'Accord every access'... remember?

> *(*THE DOCTOR *turns, and starts to look round the room.)*

BEN: We're looking for Polly.

LESTERSON: Well, she isn't here! And I haven't seen her.

BEN: Well she's been kidnapped.

LESTERSON: It sounds a little unlikely.

BEN: Oh it does, does it? Well, we've got this note which tells us so.

LESTERSON: I'm very sorry, but I... don't know anything about it.

THE DOCTOR: Lesterson?

LESTERSON: Yes?

THE DOCTOR: You haven't been building Daleks, have you?

> *(*LESTERSON *stares at* THE DOCTOR*.)*

LESTERSON: Built? No, I wouldn't know how to begin.

THE DOCTOR: And there were only three in the capsule?

LESTERSON: Yes.

THE DOCTOR: Well we've just seen *four*. One in the Governor's office and three in the corridor!

LESTERSON: But that's not possible!

THE DOCTOR: There's only one explanation. The Daleks are reproducing themselves!

(JANLEY *laughs.* LESTERSON *stares at* THE DOCTOR, *then picks up the* DALEK'*s list of materials that he showed to* JANLEY.)

JANLEY: The things are machines. How could they reproduce?

THE DOCTOR: Machines! What makes you think they're just machines. The Daleks are brilliant engineers. Nothing is beyond them, given the right materials.

LESTERSON: What?

THE DOCTOR: I said nothing is beyond them given the right materials. Lesterson... what's the matter?

(LESTERSON *stares at* THE DOCTOR *and then crumples the list in his hand. He buries his face in his hands.* THE DOCTOR *goes over and puts a hand on his shoulder.* LESTERSON *rocks backwards and forwards on a stool, in a state of shock, as the realisation of what he has done hits him.*)

JANLEY: Leave him alone. He's just been over-working, that's all.

BEN: Well, he looks bad.

JANLEY: Will you both go away. Guard! You... badgering him with questions. You've done nothing but hound him ever since you arrived on Vulcan.

(A GUARD *comes into the laboratory.*)

Bragen's orders were that nobody was to be admitted.

GUARD: Yes, but I thought it was the Ex...

JANLEY: He attacked Lesterson. Get them out of here. Both of them.

BEN : We did not attack...

JANLEY: Out, do you hear!

               (The GUARD *hustles* THE DOCTOR *and* BEN *to the door.)*

BEN: All right, all right.

               (As soon as they have gone, JANLEY *goes over to the communicator and picks up the receiver.* LESTERSON *sits on the stool, his face still buried in his hands.* JANLEY *speaks quietly into the receiver.)*

JANLEY: Janley here. Tell Valmar to come over to the lab right away. Good.

               (She replaces the receiver and goes over to LESTERSON. *She leads him over to a couch and helps him to lie down.)*

               Now, it's all right. Come on, rest here. There, you've been doing far too much. Sssh.

               *(*LESTERSON *does as he is told, too shocked to argue.* JANLEY *crosses to the bench, pours a glass of water, and empties some powder from a small bottle into it. She stirs it, goes back to* LESTERSON *and helps him drink from the glass. The* GUARD *and* VALMAR *appear in the doorway.* JANLEY *nods to the* GUARD *and he allows* VALMAR *to enter.* LESTERSON *finishes drinking and lies back on the couch.* JANLEY *takes the glass back to the bench.)*

               I've sedated him.

VALMAR: What's the matter with him?

JANLEY: Overwork, I suppose. He just suddenly broke up. Anyway, it'll give you a chance to lay in the new power cable the Daleks have asked for.

VALMAR: You don't miss a trick, do you?

(JANLEY *smiles at him, and crosses to the capsule.*)

JANLEY: We're going to lay in the new cables you wanted.

(*The capsule door opens and a* DALEK *appears.*)

DALEK: Good.

VALMAR: You're sure this is okay, Janley?

JANLEY: Of course. We help them. They help us.

DALEK: Yes. We are your ser-vants.

JANLEY: Don't take too long about it, Valmar. You saw the notice, did you?

VALMAR: I saw it.

(JANLEY *watches* VALMAR *go into the capsule.*)

5. A CORRIDOR.

(BEN *fidgets impatiently, while* THE DOCTOR *examines the notice board once more.*)

BEN: We're still no nearer finding Polly. What are we 'anging about here for?

(THE DOCTOR *consults the notebook he is holding, looks at the board and writes something down.*)

THE DOCTOR: I've found a message in code. It's an anagram, you just take the capital letters, see, work it out yourself.

BEN: I can't do crosswords.

THE DOCTOR: Meeting... tonight... 2000 hours... R - O - C - K - E - T... Rocket... R - O - O - M... Room P. Rocket Room P. It's the rebels way of calling a meeting. Only tonight we're going to be there... early.

BEN: Yeah, maybe we're nearer finding Polly than I thought.

6. *ROCKET ROOM (NIGHT)*.

(THE DOCTOR and BEN have found a hiding place in the room and are waiting for the first of the rebels to arrive.)

BEN: Cor! I've got pins and needles now.

THE DOCTOR: What is the time?

BEN: Time we went 'ome!

(BEN leans forward and rubs his leg to ease the slight cramp. THE DOCTOR hears a sound and grips BEN's arm. They crouch down again into hiding. JANLEY, KEBBLE and some other people enter the room. One by one they seat themselves round a large table in the centre of the room. VALMAR is the last to come in, and behind him is a DALEK. JANLEY has a holdall with her, in which is a case. She places the holdall on a table. VALMAR and JANLEY take the case out and open it. Inside is a DALEK gun-stick, with a long wire attachment. At the end of the wire is a remote control button. VALMAR starts to attach the gun-stick to the DALEK. Someone knocks at the door. JANLEY goes over to the door and opens it. A man enters, but the room is in semi-darkness and he remains shrouded in shadow. The man sits at the head of the table. JANLEY goes to the other end of the table, but remains standing.)

JANLEY: Now, we're going to demonstrate something. You

section leaders can pass on what you see. So far, we've been concerned with testing the strength of the Governor with a few acts of sabotage. But now, we're ready to take over.

KEBBLE: What is that thing? I've seen them moving about, but all we've been told is it's a machine Lesterson discovered.

JANLEY: Valmar?

(VALMAR steps back from the DALEK, holding the remote control button.)

VALMAR: Lesterson removed the armaments of the Daleks he discovered. I've rearmed this one, but with a controlling device. We can regulate the firepower and turn it off and on whenever we choose.

(JANLEY looks at the man in the shadows.)

JANLEY: Shall we have the demonstration now?

(The man nods in agreement. THE DOCTOR and BEN are still crouched down, but can see what is happening.)

BEN: That's the one we want. He must be the boss of this outfit.

THE DOCTOR: Sssh!

(BEN turns back to look, and THE DOCTOR absent-mindedly takes out his recorder and is about to play it. BEN sees him, reacts in horror, and manages to stop him just in time. THE DOCTOR realises the magnitude of his error, gives a suitably apologetic reaction to BEN, and pockets the recorder. Meanwhile, in the centre of the room, JANLEY adjusts

a metal plate on a stand and moves back to the table.
VALMAR *stands just behind the* DALEK, *holding the*
control.)

JANLEY: This screen is a two inch thick tungsten steel. Right.

VALMAR: Fire at the screen.

                 *(*VALMAR *places one hand on top of the* DALEK *and*
                 taps. The DALEK *fires its gun and the screen shat-*
                 ters. The people in the room react excitedly, all
                 except the man in the shadows.)

JANLEY: Quiet! You must keep quiet. We're too vulnerable
                 here.

KEBBLE: But, you can't control a thing like that. It'll turn on us!

JANLEY: No it won't.

KEBBLE: I wouldn't let any of my group go anywhere near it.

                 (There is a murmur from the crowd, generally in
                 agreement with KEBBLE.*)*

VALMAR: I can control it.

KEBBLE: Prove it.

                 *(*VALMAR *looks at* JANLEY.*)*

                 You daren't! I'm not talking about that thing firing at
                 the wall or bits of metal or anything. I mean people.
                 Have you tested whether you can stop it from killing
                 people. Our people?

VALMAR: Look, I can show you what I've done here...

KEBBLE: Forget it. How do you know a Dalek can tell the
                 difference between the Governor's people and our
                 people?

VALMAR: But I can tell the difference, you fool! And I control it.

KEBBLE: We want something better than words.

            (JANLEY *goes and stands in front of the screen.*)

JANLEY: Test it on me. Will that satisfy you?

KEBBLE: Well yes, but...

            (BEN *stares in horror and whispers to* THE DOCTOR.)

BEN: She's out of her mind!

            (*There is no reaction from* THE DOCTOR, *just an increase in the size of his frown.* JANLEY *stands in front of the screen. The* DALEK *raises its eye-stick and looks at her.* KEBBLE *leans forward, the others are frozen to the spot, their faces alive with anticipation.* VALMAR *looks at the man in the shadows.*)

VALMAR: Is it all right?

            (*Everyone stares at him, trying to make out his reaction. The man hesitates, then slowly raises his arm to indicate that they should continue.* VALMAR *looks nervously at the* DALEK.)

            When I tell you to fire...

DALEK: I am your ser-vant.

            (VALMAR *places a hand on top of the* DALEK. *He taps its dome, while his other hand presses the control button. The* DALEK's *gun-stick whirs, but it is a subtly different kind of sound from the usual one. The whirring stops, and* KEBBLE *and the others crowd*

around VALMAR, *offering their congratulations.*
JANLEY *steps forward, considerably relieved that she*
is still alive.)

JANLEY: Get back to your places.

KEBBLE: Are you all right?

JANLEY: Of course. I don't take needless risks.

VALMAR: Well done, Janley.

JANLEY: You haven't disarmed the Dalek!

(They all look around at the DALEK.*)*

Go on. Take the gun away. We don't want any acci-
dents.

(VALMAR looks at her and gives a narrow smile.
JANLEY *turns to* KEBBLE.*)*

Now, what about the girl?

KEBBLE: We've got her safely locked up. Never fear.

(BEN turns excitedly to THE DOCTOR.*)*

BEN: Hear that? Maybe they'll say where she is.

(BEN leans forward to get a better look at the
rebels. As he moves, his arm catches a loose box,
which clatters to the floor. Everyone at the table
hears the sound.)

JANLEY: Who's there?

BEN: You stay there, I'll distract them. Find out where
Polly is.

(THE DOCTOR tries to pull BEN *back, but* BEN *leaps*
out from his hiding place and runs for the door. At

once the DALEK *trains its gun on him, but* JANLEY *steps out in front of the* DALEK.)

JANLEY: No! Kebble, stop!

(As BEN *reaches the door,* KEBBLE *picks up something heavy from the table and strikes him down. He falls unconscious at* KEBBLE's *feet.)*

The guards will have heard that. Come on, we've got to get out of here.

(The rebels get up from the table in panic. They all start to leave except the man in the shadows. JANLEY *points at* BEN.)

Take him and lock him up. Quick... out!

*(*KEBBLE *and another man pick up* BEN *and carry him out of the room.* JANLEY *follows.* THE DOCTOR *is now left alone in the room with the mystery man and the* DALEK. *The* DALEK *turns around and heads straight for* THE DOCTOR's *hiding place. It stops in front of him, its gun-stick pointed directly at him. The man in the shadows steps forward - it is* BRAGEN!)

BRAGEN: You might as well come out. We know you're there.

*(*THE DOCTOR *slowly emerges from his hiding place.)*

THE DOCTOR: Bragen!

BRAGEN: Of course. Who else is fitted to be leader of the rebels?

(The DALEK *continues to train its weapon on* THE DOCTOR.)

THE DOCTOR: No doubt you want to be the leader of the Daleks too.

BRAGEN: I am the leader of the Daleks.

              (The DALEK *raises its gun.)*

THE DOCTOR: Well see if you can stop this one from killing me.

BRAGEN: Stop.

              (The DALEK *does not move.)*

              You heard me, that is an order. Turn away. Fetch the guard.

              (The DALEK *appears ready for a contest of wills. Then it drops its gun-stick and backs away.)*

DALEK: I... o-bey.

              (It glides to the door.)

THE DOCTOR: You have to have it both ways, Bragen. But how will you look in front of the Governor, when I explain your dual role to him?

BRAGEN: The Governor will hardly listen to an impostor.

THE DOCTOR: An impostor? How do you propose to prove that?

BRAGEN: My guards are now going to produce the body of the real Examiner from the mercury swamp.

THE DOCTOR: The one you murdered.

BRAGEN: The one you pretended to be.

THE DOCTOR: Murder's a far worse crime than impersonation.

BRAGEN: Yes, but you can't prove I'm a murderer, while I can prove that you're an impostor.

              (The DALEK *returns with two guards, followed by* JANLEY.*)*

Take this man away, detain him.

(THE DOCTOR is escorted away by the guards.)

JANLEY: A dangerous man.

BRAGEN: Now the only one left is the Governor.

JANLEY: Perhaps we should have dealt with the Examiner earlier.

BRAGEN: I will deal with him in time... and Quinn.

7. A PRISON CELL.

(QUINN is sitting in the cell, eating from a plate. He looks up at the sound of footsteps. Two guards approach, escorting THE DOCTOR to an adjacent cell. The first guard gets out a small box from his pocket and, holding it near the door to the cell, operates a control. A high-pitched whistle is emitted and the door springs open. THE DOCTOR watches this with interest. He steps into the cell and the guard closes the door, which automatically locks itself. The guards move away.)

QUINN: You're the last man I expected to see here.

THE DOCTOR: Works by sound, does it?

(THE DOCTOR examines the lock. He continues to do so, only half-listening to QUINN.)

QUINN: I'm speaking to you, Examiner.

THE DOCTOR: Oh, I'm sorry.

QUINN: If you'd listened to me in the first place, you wouldn't be locked up here now.

THE DOCTOR: Well your imprisonment hasn't been entirely wasted... It's brought your enemy out into...

QUINN: Bragen? I've known that all along.

THE DOCTOR: Yes, but er... did you know that he was the leader of the rebels?

QUINN: Bragen? The leader?

THE DOCTOR: Yes... It's quite a simple sort of lock, really...

QUINN: Hensell's trouble is that he thinks he can run this colony on his personality alone.

> (THE DOCTOR *starts to search through his pockets. He cannot find what he is looking for and continues to take vast amounts of obscure articles from his many pockets, putting them on the bed.*)

THE DOCTOR: But even if he knew of the dangers, could he do anything? The rebels are well organised.

QUINN: The Governor's popular. He can count on the mine workers on the perimeter for support.

THE DOCTOR: Then in that case we must get word to him.

QUINN: If you'd done your job properly, Examiner, you wouldn't be here now, and I'd have been out too.

THE DOCTOR: Ah yes, but then... I'm not the *real* Examiner.

> (QUINN *stares at* THE DOCTOR, *who is still busy examining the lock.*)

Ben, Polly and I... we're... we're just travellers, that's all. I found the Examiner, dead... Bragen murdered him.

QUINN: Everything leads back to Bragen. Just give me a chance to get my hands on him.

THE DOCTOR: We won't have that chance, unless we can get out of here.

QUINN: There's just a little matter of the cell door.

(THE DOCTOR nods and continues to examine it.)

8. LESTERSON'S LABORATORY.

(LESTERSON is still lying on the couch. He moves fitfully, gradually comes round and sits up slowly. The sleeping draught is still having an effect. He gets up and half staggers over to the work bench, where he wets a handkerchief from the tap and applies it to his face. As he is doing this a DALEK comes out of the capsule, just as a SECOND DALEK comes in through the laboratory door. LESTERSON keeps out of sight.)

SECOND DALEK: You sent for me?

FIRST DALEK: Take up a po-sit-ion at the com-mun-ic-at-ions room. Watch and re-port.

SECOND DALEK: I o-bey.

(The SECOND DALEK turns round and exits.)

LESTERSON: They're conspiring together! Oh, why didn't I realise? The Examiner was right. They are evil!

(Two more DALEKS come out of the capsule and join the other one. The three DALEKS glide out of the laboratory together.)

There are four. They can't be reproducing!

(LESTERSON moves out from behind the bench and moves fearfully towards the capsule. He makes up his mind and enters the capsule.)

9. *Interior the Capsule.*

(LESTERSON *moves into the capsule. Ahead of him is a lighted tunnel that dips down and then bends away. He moves down the tunnel. A door closes behind him, shutting him off from the laboratory. At the end of the tunnel,* LESTERSON *emerges and looks around. He sees a window and goes over to look through it. He recoils in shock at the scene before him. A* DALEK *stands in front of a bank of flashing instruments. Another* DALEK *is operating other controls nearby. A conveyor belt moves through an archway, and on it there is a continuing stream of* DALEK *bases. As each* DALEK *base reaches the end of the conveyor belt, a* DALEK *with a large scoop fitted to its sucker-stick puts a* DALEK *mutant into it. The top section of the* DALEK *is then lowered down on top of the base.* LESTERSON *stares in disbelief as he realises what is happening.)*

FIRST DALEK: Da-lek nine com-plete.

SECOND DALEK: Check.

FIRST DALEK: Da-lek ten com-plete.

SECOND DALEK: Check.

FIRST DALEK: Da-lek e-lev-en com-plete.

DALEKS: We are the hu-mans' en-e-my...

                 (As more and more DALEKS *come off the conveyor belt, they join in. Soon their words are lost in a cacophony of sound.)*

We are the hu-mans' en-e-my...

EPISODE FIVE

1. Interior the Capsule (Night).

(LESTERSON moves into the capsule. Ahead of him is a lighted tunnel that dips down and then bends away. He moves down the tunnel. A door closes behind him, shutting him off from the laboratory. At the end of the tunnel, LESTERSON emerges and looks around. He sees a window and goes over to look through it. He recoils in shock at the scene before him. A DALEK stands in front of a bank of flashing instruments. Another DALEK is operating other controls nearby. A conveyor belt moves through an archway, and on it there is a continuing stream of DALEK bases. As each DALEK base reaches the end of the conveyor belt, a DALEK with a large scoop fitted to its sucker-stick puts a DALEK mutant into it. The top section of the DALEK is then lowered down on top of the base. LESTERSON stares in disbelief as he realises what is happening.)

2. Lesterson's Laboratory.

(LESTERSON stumbles out of the capsule, half-

crazed with fear. His first thought is to try to block up the entrance to the capsule and he frantically pushes and shoves a heavy, but movable, cabinet, until it is in front of the entrance to the capsule. He leans against it, exhausted by his efforts, but feeling that he has gained a short breathing space. JANLEY *enters the laboratory and stops short when she sees* LESTERSON.)

JANLEY: What's the matter? What is it?

(LESTERSON *stares at her, his eyes wild, but does not reply.* JANLEY *goes over to* LESTERSON.)

Are you ill?

LESTERSON: Making themselves... duplicating!

JANLEY: What? What are you talking about?

(LESTERSON *breaks away and stumbles over to the generator panel.*)

LESTERSON: I started this. Opening the capsule.

(*He pulls down a lever and frantically starts to turn off all the switches and levers.* JANLEY *goes over and tries to pull him away from the panel, but* LESTERSON *shakes her off.*)

JANLEY: Lesterson!

LESTERSON: Don't try and stop me!

(JANLEY *pulls back, surprised at* LESTERSON's *passionate outburst. The various lights on the panel all die out as* LESTERSON *completes the shutdown of power.*)

JANLEY: What's happened?

LESTERSON: They forget that I control them.

               (He turns triumphantly to JANLEY, *a mad gleam in his eyes.)*

               I gave them life back again. Now I've taken it away. Finished. Stopped them.

JANLEY: The Daleks?

LESTERSON: Evil... horrible! I know what I'm going to do... laser torches. Melt then down. I'm going to melt the Daleks down to pools of metal.

JANLEY: You won't, Lesterson.

LESTERSON: Do you think I care what you can do? Tell everybody I was responsible for Resno's death. I don't care. I'm going to... wipe out the Daleks.

               *(*JANLEY *gives him one final look and hurries out of the laboratory.* LESTERSON *calls after her.)*

               Yes, tell everybody all about Resno. I'm still going to... I'm going to... wipe out the Daleks. Yes.

               (He goes over to the communications panel and lifts the receiver.)

               Get me the Examiner... Prison? Who put him there? But I've got to talk to him... I've got to, don't you understand? Please!

               *(*LESTERSON *shouts into the receiver. He stares at it as it goes dead. Behind him, the cabinet blocking the capsule entrance has been moved to one side. One of the unarmed* DALEKS *glides silently out and slowly approaches* LESTERSON *from behind.* LESTERSON *suddenly senses something behind him and turns slowly round. He stares straight into the*

eye-stick of the DALEK.)

How did you get here? I cut off the power.

DALEK: We can store po-wer. We will soon have our own.

LESTERSON: Own power?

DALEK: Why was the cap-sule door closed?

(LESTERSON edges away towards the laboratory door.)

LESTERSON: Own power? No!

(The DALEK's *eye-stick follows* LESTERSON. *He reaches the door and runs blindly down the corridor. A second, unarmed* DALEK *comes out of the capsule.)*

FIRST DALEK: Seal off the cap-sule's sec-ret ent-rance.

SECOND DALEK: I o-bey.

(The SECOND DALEK *re-enters the capsule. The other* DALEK *moves towards the laboratory door.)*

FIRST DALEK: Wait.

(The SECOND DALEK *pauses at the entrance to the capsule and turns its eye-stick back towards the* FIRST DALEK.)

No more than three Da-leks to be seen to-geth-er at a-ny one time.

SECOND DALEK: I o-bey.

FIRST DALEK: We are not rea-dy yet to teach these hu-man be-ings the law of the Da-leks.

(The SECOND DALEK *moves into the capsule.)*

3. A CORRIDOR.

(A GUARD *is on patrol in the corridor.* LESTERSON *stumbles wildly into view.)*

LESTERSON: Here! You can help me...

GUARD: What's the matter?

LESTERSON: Where's the Examiner? I've...

GUARD: The Examiner's in prison.

*(*LESTERSON *stares at the* GUARD.*)*

LESTERSON: Oh yes, I forgot.

*(*LESTERSON *turns and runs back the way he came. The* GUARD *hurries after him.)*

GUARD: What's the matter with you? What are you running for? Hey!

4. LESTERSON'S LABORATORY.

*(*JANLEY *and* KEBBLE *hustle* POLLY *into the lab. A* DALEK *comes out of the capsule.* POLLY*'s hands are tied and there is a gag around her mouth.)*

JANLEY: Did Lesterson come back?

DALEK: No.

(The DALEK *moves to inspect* POLLY.*)*

Why is this hu-man re-strict-ed?

JANLEY: She is against the Daleks.

*(*JANLEY *removes* POLLY*'s gag.* KEBBLE *gets a glass of water for her and crosses back to* POLLY. *He removes the cord from her wrists.)*

Not afraid, are you? Nothing's going to happen to you... if you behave.

(POLLY rubs her sore wrists, then takes the water. As she drinks, she stares at the DALEK.)

POLLY: Of the Daleks? Of course I am afraid. And so should you be.

JANLEY: The Daleks are going to help us.

POLLY: *Us* being the rebels, I suppose.

JANLEY: If you like.

POLLY: And when you've won, the Daleks'll just go back to being servants again? You're bigger fools than I thought.

DALEK: We are your ser-vants.

POLLY: While it suits you.

JANLEY: You'll see.

(KEBBLE urges POLLY towards the capsule. The DALEK glides away.)

KEBBLE: In! You want me to stay with her?

JANLEY: Yes, you may have to help Valmar. He'll be here in a minute to... fix up the new Dalek power cable.

KEBBLE :   Right.

DALEK: When will the work be com-plet-ed?

JANLEY: What is this cable you Daleks are laying, anyway?

DALEK: Da-leks op-er-ate on sta-tic el-ect-ric-it-y.

JANLEY: Static? Is that possible?

DALEK: To cre-ate sta-tic, the Da-leks need a com-plete ca-ble cir-cuit.

JANLEY: I see. You convert our electricity into your own power.

DALEK: That is cor-rect. When will the hu-man be-ing com-plete the work?

JANLEY: He'll be here. It's easier now. There's no-one to interfere with our plans.

5. A Prison Cell.

(THE DOCTOR *and* QUINN *are still imprisoned in adjacent barred cells.* THE DOCTOR *is sat on a bed and seems to be completely engrossed with mak-ing a glass vibrate by rubbing its rim. It is clearly getting on* QUINN'S *nerves.*)

QUINN: Do you have to do that? I'm afraid you'll find these locks are foolproof.

(THE DOCTOR *turns and looks at him.*)

THE DOCTOR: I wonder how they're converting the power.

QUINN: Converting? What are you talking about?

THE DOCTOR: The Daleks... they're powered by static electricity... it's like blood to them... a constant life-stream.

QUINN: Static isn't workable.

THE DOCTOR: It is to the Daleks. They've conquered static, just as they've conquered anti-magnetics.

(QUINN *stares at* THE DOCTOR *for a moment, then turns away.*)

QUINN: I'll not listen to anymore of this nonsense!

(THE DOCTOR shrugs and returns to the glass.)

THE DOCTOR: I don't seem to be able to hit the right note...

(He looks around the cell, glances at a water jug and a moment later gives a loud cry. THE DOCTOR scrambles to his feet and goes to get the water jug. He pours some water into the glass and then 'pings' the glass. He nods thoughtfully and then takes a sip of water, again 'pinging' the glass. THE DOCTOR continues to pour, sip and 'ping' until the water jug is empty. He shakes his head disconsolately and looks at QUINN, who has been growing more and more exasperated by THE DOCTOR's actions.)

Do you have any more water?

QUINN: I hope not... no.

(He draws a deep breath and looks at the water jug by his own bed. It is empty.)

THE DOCTOR: Then I shall have to get some.

(Just outside there is the sound of angry voices. A moment later, LESTERSON appears, struggling with a GUARD.)

SECOND GUARD: But you can't...

LESTERSON: Please. It's important... it's desperately important!

SECOND GUARD: But Bragen gave orders...

LESTERSON: Just get out of my way!

(LESTERSON shoves the GUARD out of the way and rushes up to the cell.)

Examiner... The Daleks!

THE DOCTOR: Yes?

          (The GUARD *recovers and, along with the other* GUARD, *who was following* LESTERSON, *they grab* LESTERSON.*)*

          They're duplicating... I've seen them. They've got their own power now. I... I can't stop them!

          (The GUARDS *immobilize* LESTERSON. *Another* GUARD *comes up and issues an order.)*

THIRD GUARD: Take him to Bragen.

          (The other two GUARDS *drag* LESTERSON *away.* QUINN *turns to see how* THE DOCTOR *will react to this, but* THE DOCTOR *innocently offers his empty water jug to the remaining* GUARD.*)*

THE DOCTOR: I say... I say. Do you think we might have a little more water?

QUINN: Is that all you can say? Lesterson fights his way down here to speak to you and all you can do is demand more water?

          (The GUARD *reappears with the jug, now full again.)*

THIRD GUARD: Get away from the door.

          *(*THE DOCTOR *does as he is told. The* GUARD *opens the door using the sonic key and* THE DOCTOR *listens to the sound the device makes. The* GUARD *puts down the water jug.)*

THE DOCTOR: Thank you.

          (The GUARD *turns and goes out, locking the door behind him.* QUINN *by now has caught onto what*

THE DOCTOR *is trying to do.)*

QUINN: Sorry about that outburst. I thought it might help the situation.

(THE DOCTOR *adds some water to the glass. He wets his forefinger and starts to run it round the rim of the glass until it produces a resonance. He pours in another small drop and repeats his actions. This time the note is very slightly lower.)*

Nearly... nearly...

(THE DOCTOR *again adds a tiny drop of water to the glass.)*

6. *THE GOVERNOR'S TERRACE ROOM.*

(BRAGEN *is working on papers at his desk. A* DALEK *is laying a cable in the far corner of the terrace. The cable runs through the entrance and out of sight. Two* GUARDS *enter with* LESTERSON, *who has obviously not been treated too gently.)*

BRAGEN: What's this?

FIRST GUARD: He tried to break in to speak with the Examiner.

LESTERSON: What is the Dalek doing?

(He stares at the DALEK as it continues to position the cable.)

BRAGEN: I thought you knew? Something to do with the emergency power supply.

LESTERSON: No, no! It's...it's a trick! I didn't ask for it!

BRAGEN: Lesterson, I've had reports...

(LESTERSON *moves towards the* DALEK.)

LESTERSON: What are you doing?

             (The DALEK *turns its eye-stick towards him.)*

DALEK: Lay-ing the new e-merg-en-cy po-wer sup-ply as you
             or-dered, mas-ter.

LESTERSON: It's... it's a lie!

BRAGEN: I've had reports of your incomprehensible behaviour.

             *(*LESTERSON *moves back to the desk.)*

LESTERSON: Yes, yes I can... I can explain. If you get rid of that!

             *(*BRAGEN *looks at the* DALEK, *which* LESTERSON *has
             gestured at.)*

BRAGEN: Finish now.

DALEK: I am your ser-vant.

             (The DALEK *glides out.* LESTERSON *watches it go.)*

LESTERSON: Where is the Governor?

BRAGEN: At the perimeter. Why?

LESTERSON: Call him. Get him back here as quickly as possible!
             We're all in terrible danger. The Examiner was right!
             He was right all the time...

             *(*JANLEY *comes out onto the terrace.)*

             Don't listen to anything she has to say. She's in
             league with the Daleks.

JANLEY: Now, now, now, now, please Lesterson. Just take
             things calmly. You're not well.

             *(*BRAGEN *nods to the* GUARD, *who brings forward a
             chair.)*

LESTERSON:	I'm perfectly well.
JANLEY:	Please, Lesterson. Please now. You ought to be in hospital. You promised me you'd report there.
LESTERSON:	I promised nothing of the kind!
JANLEY:	Don't you remember? Well never mind, I understand.
BRAGEN:	Pity. It's probably only temporary.
LESTERSON:	You're trying to say I'm mad!
JANLEY:	No, of course not.
BRAGEN:	No... not mad.
LESTERSON:	But I tell you, I saw the Daleks. They *were* duplicating! Bragen, I saw it, I swear to you.

(BRAGEN *looks at* JANLEY.)

JANLEY:	He suddenly started saying these things in the lab. I'm... I'm afraid...
LESTERSON:	No... No!

(BRAGEN *and* JANLEY *both look at him.*)

BRAGEN:	Keep him under restraint.

(LESTERSON *backs away, but is grabbed by the* GUARD *behind him.* LESTERSON *sags helplessly, anguish etched on his face.*)

LESTERSON:	Won't nobody listen to me?

7. *INTERIOR THE CAPSULE.*

(POLLY *is sitting on the floor of one of the inner compartments within the capsule. The floor is a mass of cables, going in all directions.* VALMAR *is busy connecting the cables to a large, square box. A* DALEK *is standing nearby.)*

VALMAR: Pass me that small screwdriver.

POLLY: I can't, my hands are tied. Anyway, I wouldn't help you even if I could.

VALMAR: Okay.

(He gets the screwdriver himself. The DALEK *moves backwards and* KEBBLE *squeezes into the compartment, carrying more cables.)*

More? I can't handle them.

KEBBLE: This is the last.

*(*POLLY *notices that the* DALEK *has now left.)*

POLLY: The Dalek's gone now.

KEBBLE: That doesn't mean you can start talking.

VALMAR: Oh, leave her alone, Kebble. She isn't doing any harm.

POLLY: You think you're very tough, don't you? Pushing a girl around. I'd like to see you come up against a real man.

KEBBLE: Like who?

POLLY: Like Ben, for instance.

KEBBLE: Don't worry about him. We've got him safely stowed away.

POLLY: You've got Ben?

KEBBLE: He's just sleeping off a slight fall.

VALMAR: I told you to leave her alone.

(KEBBLE *glares at* VALMAR.)

POLLY: Your name's Valmar, isn't it?

VALMAR: That's it.

POLLY: You want the Daleks to fight the Governor. But don't you see? They'll turn on you too.

KEBBLE: What? Three big pepper-pots?

VALMAR: One of them *did* kill Resno, and you saw what the Dalek did to that sheet of metal.

POLLY: And that's just the beginning.

KEBBLE: Don't listen to her. She's giving you the Examiner's line.

(POLLY *looks at* VALMAR.)

POLLY: He isn't the Examiner. We're just travellers... landed here by accident. The Doctor, that's the man you think is the Examiner, found the real Examiner dead and picked up his papers.

(KEBBLE *laughs disbelievingly.* VALMAR *carries on with his work, but looks at* POLLY.)

VALMAR: This Doctor of yours. He... knows something about the Daleks?

POLLY: He's tried to warn everyone. That's the only reason we stayed here.

(POLLY *suddenly looks up. The* DALEK *has returned and is looking into the compartment.*)

DALEK: When will the work be com-plet-ed?

VALMAR: I don't know. I'll need a new junction box... Like this one.

(The DALEK *glides out again.)*

POLLY: You've all underestimated these Daleks.

KEBBLE: Better brains than us, I suppose?

POLLY: I only know what the Doctor has told me. He says they are capable of exterminating whole nations.

VALMAR: Perhaps. But what would they want to kill us for... after we've taken over. We're friendly with the Daleks.

POLLY: Don't you see, human beings can't be friends with Daleks. They don't have friends.

VALMAR: I don't see why not.

POLLY: It's a kind of hatred for anything unlike themselves. They think they're superior.

*(*VALMAR *looks at* KEBBLE.)*

VALMAR: The girl's got something.

KEBBLE: You want to tell Janley? You're welcome!

POLLY: Janley! She'll betray the lot of you, if she gets the chance.

*(*VALMAR *turns back to his work as the* DALEK *reappears.)*

DALEK: The oth-er junc-tion box is out-side.

VALMAR: Thank you.

(The DALEK *glides away.* VALMAR *continues his work.* KEBBLE *grins at* POLLY. *He bends forwards to her, confidentially.)*

KEBBLE: Talk too much, don't you? Didn't you know he was soft on Janley?

(VALMAR *looks up threateningly.*)

All right, all right... I'm just putting her straight.

(VALMAR *turns back to his work.*)

VALMAR: More slack on the cables.

(KEBBLE *pulls in the cables, amused by the situation.*)

8. *A CORRIDOR.*

(*A* DALEK *moves slowly down the corridor, a cable draped over its sucker-stick. A* GUARD, *stationed by the notice board, watches.* HENSELL *comes into view and starts to walk down the corridor. As he does, the* DALEK *moves out of sight round a bend.*)

HENSELL: What are all these cables lying about?

GUARD: New emergency power supply.

HENSELL: Who's idea was that?

GUARD: What do you want to know for?

HENSELL: What do I...? Don't you know I'm the Governor!

(*The* GUARD *immediately stands to attention.*)

Where are you from?

GUARD: The interior, sir.

HENSELL: The interior? Why are you carrying a gun?

GUARD: I'm a squad leader in Bragen's guard, sir.

HENSELL: Oh I see. Bragen's guard, eh! All right. Carry on.

(HENSELL, white with fury, strides down the corridor. The GUARD *gives a sigh of relief and leans back against the notice board.)*

9. A PRISON CELL.

(A GUARD *comes to investigate the noise* THE DOCTOR *is making with the glass.)*

GUARD: Cut that noise you two!

(Without warning, the door to QUINN'*s cell suddenly clicks open. As the* GUARD *rushes forward,* THE DOCTOR *throws the remaining contents of the water jug in his face. The* GUARD *is taken by surprise and* QUINN *has time to get out of his cell. He struggles with the* GUARD, THE DOCTOR *cheering him on.* QUINN *knocks the* GUARD *out, and takes his sonic key. He operates it and the door of* THE DOCTOR'*s cell opens.* QUINN *drags the* GUARD *inside the cell.* THE DOCTOR *takes the key and operates it, comparing it with a note from his recorder.* THE DOCTOR *starts to leave his cell, then turns back in again.)*

QUINN: Come on.

THE DOCTOR: Wait a minute.

*(*THE DOCTOR *comes back out again, this time holding the water jug.)*

We don't want him trying it...

(He glances down at the GUARD.*)*

Although he seemed a bit tone deaf to me.

*(*QUINN *hauls* THE DOCTOR *away from the door, and activates the lock.)*

10. THE GOVERNOR'S TERRACE ROOM.

(BRAGEN is seated at the desk, reading some papers. HENSELL walks in. BRAGEN looks up, surprised, and, out of habit, starts to get up. He stops himself, and sits back down again, and, with a look of insolence on his face, continues to read.)

HENSELL: Well Bragen, these trip are becoming more and more demanding.

BRAGEN: I didn't expect you, Governor.

HENSELL: Oh, I had as much as I could stand. Well, what's been happening here?

BRAGEN: One moment.

(He continues to read. HENSELL, a reasonable man, nevertheless starts to get irritable at this insubordination.)

HENSELL: I asked you a question, man.

BRAGEN: I heard you.

HENSELL: Look, your work can wait. You can hand over to me tomorrow. I want to hear about the Examiner.

(BRAGEN finishes reading, carefully signs his name at the bottom of the sheet, and sits back in the chair.)

BRAGEN: The Examiner is at present in gaol!

HENSELL: In gaol? That's rather dangerous isn't it? Who put him there?

BRAGEN: I did.

HENSELL: You did? For heaven's sake, why?

BRAGEN: He's an impostor, Governor... possibly a murderer as well. We've just discovered the body of the *real* Examiner in the mercury swamp.

HENSELL: I hope you're sure of your facts, Bragen?

BRAGEN: Quite sure.

HENSELL: This could have... far-reaching consequences.

BRAGEN: As far as I am concerned, there's nothing more to be said. Now if there is nothing further?

(He settles down to work again, effectively trying to dismiss HENSELL.*)*

HENSELL: Nothing further! Who the devil do you think you're talking to. Stand up when you're speaking to me man!

BRAGEN: I prefer to remain seated.

HENSELL: Do you now. We'll soon see about that. Guards!

(Two guards enter and stand to attention by the door.)

Take this man out of my office!

(The guards do not move.)

Did you hear what I said? That is an order!

(The guards still do not move.)

BRAGEN: You forget, my dear Hensell, they are not your guards, they are mine.

HENSELL: I am the Governor.

BRAGEN: No... not now... I am.

(He leans back, enjoying every moment of

HENSELL'*s humiliation.)*

HENSELL: I see... Your guards, eh? Yes, Quinn warned me about your guards. But we all took them too lightly, didn't we? But we'll soon change that.

(He goes to the door. The guards move to bar his way. HENSELL *turns back to* BRAGEN.*)*

You imbecile! How long do you think your handful of guards can hang out when the people hear that I am being kept a prisoner in my own capital?

BRAGEN: The people will do exactly as they are told, Hensell.

(He presses a button on the desk and stands up.)

It will of course be easier for them if you co-operate with us.

(He leaves the desk, proffering the seat to HENSELL. *A* DALEK *enters.)*

Wait there. Guards... dismiss.

HENSELL: So Bragen, you want my cooperation, do you?

BRAGEN: It would save bloodshed. I might even let you keep the title of Governor.

HENSELL: Might you now! I'll tell you what you *will* do. You'll order your guards to disarm and place yourself under arrest, *immediately!*

BRAGEN: So... you reject my offer? I thought it a generous one in the circumstances.

HENSELL: What circumstances?

BRAGEN: Look at this.

(He unwraps a DALEK *gun-stick.)*

HENSELL: What is it?

BRAGEN: The reason that the colony is now mine.

             (*He crosses to the* DALEK *and attaches the gun-stick into its socket.* HENSELL, *sensing danger, is suddenly nervous.*)

HENSELL: Is it a... a weapon of some kind?

BRAGEN: I'll arrange a demonstration for you. Do you still refuse my offer?

HENSELL: I will not be intimidated.

BRAGEN: No, of course not. In character to the last, Hensell.

             (*Without taking his eyes off* HENSELL, BRAGEN *barks an order to the* DALEK.)

             Kill him!

             (*The* DALEK'*s gun-stick rattles.* HENSELL *half-rises from his desk and collapses across it, dead.* BRAGEN *snatches the gun-stick from the* DALEK *and moves over to examine the body.*)

DALEK: Why do hu-man be-ings kill hu-man be-ings?

BRAGEN: Get on with your work.

DALEK: Yes, mas-ter. I o-bey.

             (*The* DALEK *glides away across the terrace.*)

BRAGEN: Yes, obey me. From now on I will have complete obedience... from everyone.

             11. LESTERSON'S LABORATORY.

             (THE DOCTOR *and* QUINN *slip into the laboratory.*

They duck behind the work bench as a DALEK *comes out of the capsule.* VALMAR *follows just behind.)*

VALMAR: I'll have to check the cable circuit now. Otherwise it's just as you asked for.

DALEK: Ve-ry well.

VALMAR: Why can't you carry on with the power you're drawing from the colony? Why go to all this trouble?

DALEK: Un-til now we have had to re-charge from the co-lo-ny sup-ply. With sta-tic po-wer, the Da-leks will be twice as... use-ful.

*(*JANLEY *hurries into the laboratory.)*

JANLEY: Valmar, quick!

VALMAR: What's the matter?

JANLEY: The Governor's back.

VALMAR: What about the girl?

JANLEY: Leave her.

(The DALEK *moves after* JANLEY *and* VALMAR.)*

DALEK: I will fol-low you.

VALMAR: What for?

DALEK: I am your ser-vant.

(They leave the laboratory. THE DOCTOR *and* QUINN *get up from behind the bench.* THE DOCTOR *immediately starts to examine the cables leading from the capsule.)*

THE DOCTOR: An electrical circuit of their own, supplying static electricity! I wonder how much longer we have got?

(He starts to follow the cables into the capsule, with QUINN *behind him.)*

12. INTERIOR THE CAPSULE.

*(*POLLY *and* KEBBLE *are inside the capsule. Both are listening.)*

THE DOCTOR
(*oov*):
I didn't realise they'd have a circuit of their own.

*(*KEBBLE *clamps a hand over* POLLY'*s mouth. She struggles and manages to shout a warning.)*

POLLY: Doctor, look out!

13. LESTERSON'S LABORATORY.

*(*KEBBLE *emerges from the capsule, carrying a wrench, just as* QUINN *and* THE DOCTOR *are going in.* KEBBLE *and* QUINN *fight, and* KEBBLE *swings the wrench viciously at* QUINN'*s head.* QUINN *manages to duck and he knocks* KEBBLE *out.* POLLY *comes rushing out.)*

POLLY: Are you all right?

THE DOCTOR: Well done! Who was the man who went outside just now?

POLLY: Valmar. He's been working for the Daleks.

THE DOCTOR: On their static power supply.

POLLY: Doctor, they've got Ben.

THE DOCTOR: Yes, I know. He ran away so that I could... Oh well, it's

a long story, but don't worry. That boy can take care
of himself...

*(THE DOCTOR turns back to the capsule. As he is
about to enter, a DALEK emerges... only this time
the DALEK is armed!)*

QUINN: Did you see that?

*(THE DOCTOR, QUINN and POLLY back towards the
laboratory door. They move slowly, and as they do
THE DOCTOR bends and picks up the wrench that
KEBBLE dropped.)*

That won't help.

THE DOCTOR: Get out, Polly.

POLLY: But, Doctor...

THE DOCTOR: Out. Go on!

*(They back to the door. The DALEK starts to move
out of the capsule. QUINN and POLLY make their
escape.)*

14. OUTSIDE LESTERSON'S LABORATORY.

*(THE DOCTOR comes out last and jams the wrench
through the handles of the laboratory doors.)*

15. LESTERSON'S LABORATORY.

SECOND DALEK: Have they es-caped?

FIRST DALEK: Yes. Re-turn to cap-sule and re-port.

SECOND DALEK: I o-bey.

(*The* FIRST DALEK *tries to push open the doors, but they remain closed. The* DALEK *aims its gun-stick at the doors and fires. The* DALEK *pushes the doors once more and they open. The twisted remnants of the wrench hang in pieces on what remains of the door handles. The* SECOND DALEK *returns to the capsule, where a whole army of* DALEKS *are now massed. The* FIRST DALEK *moves off down the corridor.*)

FIRST DALEK: We are to wait here un-til the hu-man be-ings fight a-mong them-selves.

SECOND DALEK: Then we will strike.

FIRST DALEK: And Ex-ter-min-ate.

DALEKS: Ex-ter-min-ate. Ex-ter-min-ate. Ex-ter-min-ate. Ex-ter-min-ate. Ex-ter-min-ate. Ex-ter-min-ate. Ex-ter-min-ate. Ex-ter-min-ate. Ex-ter-min-ate. Ex-ter-min-ate. Ex-ter-min-ate. Ex-ter-min-ate.

16. THE GOVERNOR'S TERRACE ROOM.

(THE DOCTOR, POLLY *and* QUINN *examine the body of* THE GOVERNOR.)

QUINN: The one man who could have saved us.

THE DOCTOR: Don't worry. The people will follow you, too.

QUINN: Maybe. But there wasn't any *maybe* about Hensell. He was old-fashioned, single-minded, yes. But he's done a lot of wonderful work for this colony. Events turned out against him, that's all. But why? Why was he killed?

BRAGEN (*oov*): I can answer that.

(BRAGEN *appears flanked by two armed guards.*)

He wanted to destroy the Daleks. So one of them killed him. Now I'm declaring martial law. You will be returned to prison... and properly guarded this time.

THE DOCTOR: Martial law! What good do you think that will do against the Daleks?

BRAGEN: The Daleks will do as I tell them.

THE DOCTOR: We shall see, shan't we.

BRAGEN: Take them away!

(*The guards lead* THE DOCTOR, POLLY *and* QUINN *away.*)

17. LESTERSON'S LABORATORY (NIGHT).

(*A continuous line of* DALEKS *pours out from the capsule. One by one they cross the laboratory and go out the door.*)

DALEKS: Ex-ter-min-ate. Ex-ter-min-ate. Ex-ter-min-ate.

SECOND DALEK: Ex-ter-min-ate all hu-mans.

FIRST DALEK: Ex-ter-min-ate all hu-mans.

SECOND DALEK: Ex-ter-min-ate... An-ni-hi-late... Des-troy. Da-leks con-quer and des-troy.

DALEKS: Da-leks con-quer and des-troy. Da-leks con-quer and des-troy...

(*The* DALEKS' *voices become an unintelligible cacophony of noise.*)

EPISODE SIX

1. LESTERSON'S LABORATORY (NIGHT).

(A continuous line of DALEKS *pours out from the capsule. One by one they cross the laboratory and go out the door.)*

SECOND DALEK: Ex-ter-min-ate all hu-mans.

FIRST DALEK: Ex-ter-min-ate all hu-mans.

SECOND DALEK: Ex-ter-min-ate... An-ni-hi-late... Des-troy. Da-leks con-quer and des-troy.

DALEKS: Da-leks con-quer and des-troy. Da-leks con-quer and des-troy...

(The DALEKS' *voices become an unintelligible cacophony of noise.)*

FIRST DALEK: Take up po-sit-ions rea-dy to ex-ter-min-ate all hu-man be-ings.

(The other DALEKS *chorus in unison.)*

DALEKS: Ex-ter-min-ate. Ex-ter-min-ate. Ex-ter-min-ate. Ex-ter-min-ate. Ex-ter-min-ate...

2. A Corridor.

(Two armed GUARDS *shepherd* THE DOCTOR, POLLY *and* QUINN *along the corridor.* THE DOCTOR *stops suddenly as a* DALEK *turns into the corridor and takes up a stationary position.)*

FIRST GUARD: Move on!

THE DOCTOR: The Dalek!

POLLY: What about it?

THE DOCTOR: Can't you see it's armed?

FIRST GUARD: Keep moving!

(The second GUARD *urges them on again from behind. The* DALEK *moves to block their path. The* GUARD *in front stops, uncertainly.)*

DALEK: This ar-e-a is re-strict-ed.

QUINN: On whose authority?

FIRST GUARD: Silence!

(The DALEK *stares at* THE DOCTOR *with its eye-stick, staring him up and down. Then it turns its attention back to the* GUARD.)*

DALEK: Re-peat. This ar-e-a is re-strict-ed.

*(*POLLY *glances behind them and grips* THE DOCTOR's *arm. He turns as another* DALEK *glides up the corridor behind them.)*

SECOND DALEK: O-bey or you shall be ex-ter-min-at-ed.

QUINN: I thought they obeyed us?

(The two GUARDS *look at each other, unsure of*

themselves.)

POLLY: What do we do now, Doctor?

(THE DOCTOR *assumes authority and the* GUARDS *follow his lead. He indicates with a nod that they should go back up the corridor. They pass the* DALEK, *which watches them carefully as they pass but does not attempt to stop them.)*

QUINN: This way.

FIRST DALEK: They will be ex-ter-min-at-ed.

3. *THE GOVERNOR'S TERRACE ROOM.*

(BRAGEN *is sitting quietly at the desk.* JANLEY *paces up and down in front of him.)*

JANLEY: We've won. The revolution is over. I'll pass the word to Valmar, Kebble and the rest.

BRAGEN: Wait. The revolution is not quite over yet.

JANLEY: What more can we do? Hensell is dead, you're the new Governor. The battle's over.

BRAGEN: Not quite. You mentioned Kebble, Valmar and that rabble. Well now they must be dealt with.

JANLEY: But those are our own men...

BRAGEN: Of course.

JANLEY: I don't understand.

BRAGEN: Do you think I can ever be secure in that chair while that rabble are still loose? They rebelled against Hensell yesterday... tomorrow it'll be my turn. Well, let them rebel. Tell them the guards have taken control. Let them attack. Then we can crush them, utterly!

JANLEY: You say "we".

BRAGEN: Yes. We have come a long way together you and I. Are you going to back down now?

4. OUTSIDE THE GOVERNOR'S TERRACE ROOM.

(VALMAR *is about to enter the terrace when he overhears this exchange. He draws back into cover and listens.*)

JANLEY (*oov*): Couldn't you just arrest them?

BRAGEN (*oov*): Everyone... must be killed.

JANLEY (*oov*): Must they all be slaughtered?

5. THE GOVERNOR'S TERRACE ROOM.

BRAGEN: All of them. Well... are you still with me?

(*Unseen by* JANLEY, BRAGEN *takes a gun out from a drawer in the desk.*)

JANLEY: I suppose so.

BRAGEN: Then do as I say.

(JANLEY *nods.* BRAGEN *smiles and tosses the gun onto the desk.*)

I'm glad you agree with me.

(JANLEY *turns, sees the gun, and realises that* BRAGEN *was quite prepared to kill her had she disagreed with him.*)

6. OUTSIDE THE GOVERNOR'S TERRACE ROOM.

(VALMAR *frowns and slips quietly away.*)

7. A CORRIDOR.

(THE DOCTOR, POLLY, QUINN *and the two* GUARDS *reach an intersection. Another* DALEK *moves down the corridor and stops between the foremost* GUARD *and the others.*)

THE DOCTOR: Now!

(THE DOCTOR *puts one hand over his eyes, and with his other hand aims a wild swipe with his recorder at the* GUARD. *Unseen by* THE DOCTOR, QUINN *knocks out the* GUARD. THE DOCTOR *takes away his hand from his eyes and, seeing the* GUARD *lying on the floor, thinks he has been successful.* POLLY *pushes aside the other* GUARD. THE DOCTOR, POLLY *and* QUINN *dodge up the corridor and make their escape.*)

8. THE REST ROOM.

(VALMAR, *armed with a gun, pushes* BEN *into the room.*)

BEN: Well, what have you brought me here for?

VALMAR: Quiet!

BEN: Whose side are you on anyway?

VALMAR: I thought I was going to be on the winning side.

BEN: What changed your mind?

VALMAR: Bragen. The colony's become too small for him. He

wants us out of the way now.

BEN: Yeah, it often happens that way, mate, when you follow blokes like him.

VALMAR: Look, I'm going to try and get your friends here, if I can. So wait here.

(VALMAR *leaves the room.*)

9. THE GOVERNOR'S TERRACE ROOM.

(*The scanner on* BRAGEN's *desk buzzes.* BRAGEN *presses a switch.*)

GUARD (*oov*): Station One reporting, Governor Bragen.

BRAGEN: Yes.

GUARD (*oov*): The rebels are gathering. We've got them under observation.

BRAGEN: Don't let them concentrate in large groups. Hit them before they organise. They'll be making their move any time now.

GUARD (*oov*): Right.

(BRAGEN *snaps off the scanner. He presses another switch.*)

BRAGEN: People of Vulcan... This is your *new* Governor talking to you. I have to announce that Governor Hensell has been murdered by the rebels. I have taken control temporarily, until order is restored. People living on the perimeter and in the interior should stay calm. We know who the murderers are.

10. THE REST ROOM.

BRAGEN (*oov*):   I shall keep you informed of events as soon as I am able, so listen for the signal to watch your communication sets. That is all.

> (BEN *turns round as* THE DOCTOR, POLLY *and* QUINN *hurry in.*)

THE DOCTOR: Ben! There you are. I knew you'd be all right!

POLLY: Ben!

BEN: Polly! Are you okay?

POLLY: Yes.

BEN: Did Valmar find you, then?

POLLY: Valmar? No.

QUINN: What's this about Valmar?

BEN: Well it seems Bragen's gone power-mad. He wants the rebels to revolt, then he can finish them off.

THE DOCTOR: The Daleks won't care who they fight. They'll exterminate every human being on this planet.

POLLY: Doctor... please let's go back to the TARDIS.

> (THE DOCTOR *moves to the door.*)

THE DOCTOR: Quinn. Keep them both here.

> (*He exits.*)

BEN: Hey... wait a minute, Doctor!

> (BEN *goes to follow, but* QUINN *stops him.*)

All right. All right.

QUINN: Now what do you think he's up to?

11. *A CORRIDOR.*

(Three DALEKS *are patrolling the corridor.)*

FIRST DALEK: Or-ders re-ceived. Da-leks com-mence ex-ter-min-at-ion.

SECOND AND

THIRD DALEKS: Ex-ter-min-ate. Ex-ter-min-ate. Ex-ter-min-ate!

(Further down the corridor KEBBLE, *two armed* GUARDS *and several other men appear, just as* THE DOCTOR *enters from another corridor.)*

KEBBLE: Just a minute, Examiner.

GUARD: All right... hold it!

THE DOCTOR: Get down everyone.

(For no apparent reason, THE DOCTOR *suddenly drops to the floor. One of the* DALEKS *at the other end of the corridor fires its gun-stick and the* GUARD *collapses, dead even before he hits the ground.* KEBBLE *crouches down. The* DALEK *fires again. Two of the men with* KEBBLE *stagger and fall.* THE DOCTOR *grabs* KEBBLE's *arm.* THE DOCTOR *and* KEBBLE *zigzag up the corridor, managing to avoid the* DALEK's *fire. They throw themselves round the corner.)*

12. *LESTERSON'S LABORATORY.*

(Three DALEKS *stand in the laboratory.* VALMAR *has just finished fitting them with control wires.* JANLEY *rushes in and then stops.* VALMAR *turns to face her, the control wires in his hand.)*

VALMAR: Don't come any nearer.

JANLEY: What do you mean?

VALMAR: I overheard your conversation with Bragen. But you can't stand up to the Daleks, so your plan will come to nothing.

JANLEY: Not my plan... Bragen's.

VALMAR: But that's the same thing.

JANLEY: Not any more.

VALMAR: You expect me to believe that?

JANLEY: Look Valmar, he was going to kill me too. I came here to do exactly what you've done. Let Bragen see what the Daleks are like. He doesn't know how strong they are.

               (VALMAR listens to her.)

               He's got to be stopped.

FIRST DALEK: You will lead us to the mid-dle of your par-ty of hu-man be-ings?

VALMAR: Yes.

FIRST DALEK: We will fight... for you.

JANLEY: Believe me, Val. It's the only way to save all our lives.

VALMAR: Did you know that the Daleks are duplicating?

JANLEY: Yes.

FIRST DALEK: But we are your friends.

SECOND DALEK: We will serve you.

THIRD DALEK: Take us to the cen-tre of your group.

VALMAR: Can we trust them?

JANLEY: We must! The guards have orders to wipe us out. We must use the Daleks. Come on.

> (JANLEY, VALMAR *and the three* DALEKS *leave the laboratory.*)

13. THE REST ROOM.

> (THE DOCTOR *runs back into the room and goes straight to the window.*)

POLLY: Doctor!

THE DOCTOR: Does it open?

BEN: I dunno.

THE DOCTOR: If it doesn't, we're done for! Up you go.

POLLY: What's happening?

THE DOCTOR: The Daleks... they're teaming all over the corridors. We've got to get back to Lesterson's lab.

> (BEN *and* QUINN *open the window and help* POLLY *out.* KEBBLE *runs through the door, but as he does he is shot and falls to the floor.* THE DOCTOR *starts to climb out of the window, just as a* DALEK *reaches the doorway.* BRAGEN'S *voice echoes from the intercom.*)

BRAGEN (*oov*):   This is Governor Bragen speaking. A group of rebels is attempting to take over the...

14. THE GOVERNOR'S TERRACE ROOM.

BRAGEN: ...colony. It is the duty of all loyal citizens to help the guards resist. Stay in your homes. Order will be restored. Listen to my bulletins.

(BRAGEN turns off the intercom. A GUARD runs onto the terrace.)

GUARD: The rebels! They're using the Daleks against our people!

BRAGEN: Well get back and fight! Why do you come running in to me? What do you think your guns are for?

GUARD: The guns don't work against them!

BRAGEN: Get back and fight them!

15. *A CORRIDOR.*

(The rebels have built a barricade, with boxes and anything else they can find. A battle rages over the barricade, between the rebels and the guards. A guard falls to the ground as a rebel fires at him. JANLEY and VALMAR appear at the head of the corridor, a DALEK between them. JANLEY holds the control wire attached to the DALEK's gun-stick.)

JANLEY: Over there...

(JANLEY points. The DALEK fires and a guard collapses.)

Over there...

(This time the DALEK ignores the order and fires at the barricade.)

No! They're *our* people!

VALMAR: Cut the Dalek gun off!

(*JANLEY presses the switch, but the DALEK continues to fire. Two rebels slump over the barricade. VAL-MAR snatches the control wire from JANLEY.*)

I told you to cut the gun off!

JANLEY: I did!

VALMAR: Our own people...

(*He pulls off the wire. The DALEK moves away and stares at them with its eye-stick. VALMAR looks from JANLEY to the DALEK.*)

JANLEY: Valmar, look at it.

DALEK: Your use-ful-ness is o-ver.

(*A guard appears down the corridor. The DALEK swings round and fires. The guard is instantly killed.*)

JANLEY: Come on!

(*JANLEY and VALMAR turn and flee.*)

Quick, Valmar. Come on!

16. LESTERSON'S LABORATORY.

(*The door opens and LESTERSON, THE DOCTOR, POLLY and BEN all hurry in. LESTERSON ushers the others behind the cover of the work bench.*)

POLLY: Doctor, it's stupid to hide in here!

BEN: D'you fancy your chances out there in the corridors? No thanks.

THE DOCTOR: The answer must be here somewhere.

LESTERSON: Ssssh!

(A DALEK *comes out of the capsule, moves across to the laboratory door and exits.)*

You must be absolutely quiet. They know everything that's going on. Everything! They even know what you're thinking.

*(*BEN *and* POLLY *look at each other.* LESTERSON's *mind has obviously been affected by all that he has gone through.)*

BEN: Where do they get their power from, Lesterson?

LESTERSON: Ah, I tried to turn the power off. But they were miles ahead of me. Marvellous creatures. You have to admire them.

BEN: Lesterson. We've got to stop them!

LESTERSON: Oh, it's too late for that. They're the new species, you see. Taking over from *homo sapiens*. Man's had his day. Finished now.

(He signals silence as the DALEK *returns, just as another* DALEK *comes out of the capsule.)*

FIRST DALEK: The sta-tic cir-cuit is near-ly com-plete.

SECOND DALEK: Soon we can a-ban-don the po-wer we are u-sing.

(From the corridor comes the sound of a DALEK's *gun and a man's dying scream.)*

FIRST DALEK: The hu-mans are be-ing ex-ter-min-at-ed.

(The two DALEKS *go into the capsule.)*

BEN: Did you hear that? They're going to use their *own* power!

THE DOCTOR: The cables they laid... the trick I tried before won't work anymore.

LESTERSON: Oh, that's no good now. We're finished. All we can do is marvel at the creatures who are taking our place.

> (LESTERSON *beams with joy as he peers over the bench.*)

> *17. A CORRIDOR.*

> (JANLEY *hurries past the top of the corridor. She stops and looks down the empty corridor.*)

VALMAR: No... no.

> (JANLEY *hurries down the corridor.* VALMAR *limps to the top of the corridor and calls after her.*)

Don't be a fool. Come on!

> (QUINN *appears behind* VALMAR *and catches his arm.*)

She's in the open that way... she'll run into...

> (VALMAR *halts as a* DALEK *glides round the other end of the corridor.* JANLEY *stops. The* DALEK *aims its gun-stick at her.*)

JANLEY: Come on. Come on.

> (QUINN *pulls* VALMAR *back round the corner.*)

> *18. LESTERSON'S LABORATORY.*

> (*A woman's scream echoes through the air.* POLLY *covers her face.* BEN *tries to comfort her.*)

BEN: Take it easy, Polly.

POLLY: Can't we do anything? They're murdering every-
                body... one by one.

                *(POLLY buries her face in her hands, weeping with
                frustration and horror. BEN turns angrily to
                LESTERSON.)*

BEN: You've done all this. Why did you give them power
                in the first place?

                *(THE DOCTOR puts a restraining arm on BEN's
                shoulder. He shakes his head and indicates that
                LESTERSON is beyond answering for his actions
                now. LESTERSON looks vaguely at BEN.)*

LESTERSON: Well, I could control it, you see. And then Janley got
                one of her men... Valmar, I think it was... yes, he
                rigged up a secret cable. It's carrying power directly
                from the colony's supply.

THE DOCTOR: Where? Where is it, Lesterson?

LESTERSON: Valmar's the only one who can answer that. Or the
                Daleks of course. They know everything. Yes, you
                should ask the Daleks...

                (LESTERSON smiles happily to himself.)

BEN: Well we must find Valmar.

THE DOCTOR: No. You stay here and look after Polly.

                *(A burst of gunfire comes from just outside the
                laboratory.)*

                19. A CORRIDOR.

                *(Two men crumple and fall dead as a DALEK fires
                at them. Another man runs up the corridor, but is*

not quick enough and falls to the floor as a DALEK *fires at him.)*

20. LESTERSON'S LABORATORY.

(A woman and a GUARD *run through the door, a* DALEK *in hot pursuit. The* DALEK *fires and kills the woman. The* GUARD *grabs the* DALEK *by its sucker-stick, but the* DALEK *throws him off and turns its gun-stick on him.)*

GUARD: No!

(The DALEK *fires and the* GUARD *dies instantly.)*

21. A CORRIDOR.

*(*VALMAR *cradles* JANLEY's *head in his arms. She is dead.* QUINN *bends down.)*

QUINN: You'll have to leave her now, Valmar.

VALMAR: She wasn't as bad as you think...

*(*THE DOCTOR *appears at the top of the corridor.)*

THE DOCTOR: Valmar!

(At the other end of the corridor, a guard staggers into view and falls dead.)

QUINN: Get down... both of you!

*(*QUINN *drags* VALMAR *down.* THE DOCTOR *lies on the ground, pulling his jacket over his head. A* DALEK *appears and glides up the corridor, examining the bodies as it goes. It appears satisfied that they are all dead, and glides away. As soon as it is out of sight,* THE DOCTOR *gets up and goes over to* VALMAR.)*

THE DOCTOR: Valmar! Where is the Dalek's power supply?

(VALMAR *looks vague, dazed.* QUINN *brings him back to reality.*)

QUINN: We've got to stop them, Valmar. She's dead! There's nothing you can do for her!

VALMAR: The main cable's inside the capsule...

(THE DOCTOR *and* QUINN *start to move off.*)

... but there's nothing you can do.

QUINN: There must be some way of cutting off the power.

THE DOCTOR: What makes you think I want to do that? We need more time. I know... a diversion. Bragen's guards. We'll have to use them to keep the Daleks busy. You go to Bragen.

22. THE GOVERNOR'S TERRACE ROOM.

(BRAGEN *is controlling operations. He snaps on one switch after another and barks orders.*)

BRAGEN: Section One... where's your report? Are you there Section One? Section Two... Section Two, why don't they answer? Can you hear me Section Two? Section Three? Oh, why don't they answer? I am their Governor. Why don't they answer?

(He bangs his fist on the desk in frustration.)

23. A CORRIDOR.

(A DALEK *stands in the foreground, its eye-stick surveying the carnage. Bodies of both guards and rebels litter the floor.*)

24. *THE REST ROOM.*

(The bodies of KEBBLE *and another man lie crumpled by the window.)*

25. *LESTERSON'S LABORATORY.*

(The bodies of the GUARD *and the woman lie on the floor.)*

26. *A CORRIDOR.*

(A DALEK *moves along the corridor. More bodies cover the floor and the* DALEK *studies them, checking to make sure that there is no further opposition.)*

27. *LESTERSON'S LABORATORY.*

*(*BEN, POLLY *and* LESTERSON *are hidden behind the work bench. A* DALEK *comes out of the capsule as* BRAGEN'*s voice issues from the intercom.)*

BRAGEN (*oov*): This is Bragen speaking. I am speaking to the Daleks. Daleks, listen to me. I am the Governor. You must work for me. Do not trust the rebels. I will give you whatever you want. But immobilise your guns. This is the Governor speaking...

BEN: He's nuts, trying to talk to the Daleks.

(As he speaks, he notices a cupboard nearby and points to it.)

Lesterson, what's in that cupboard?

LESTERSON: Nothing. It's quite empty.

BEN: Well, come on, Polly. We'll be safe in there, love.

            (They get into the cupboard.)

            28. THE GOVERNOR'S TERRACE ROOM.

            (BRAGEN is still speaking into the intercom.)

BRAGEN: Do you hear me, Daleks? You will obey my orders.

            (QUINN appears. He has a gun in his hand.)

QUINN: No use, Bragen. The Daleks have stopped obeying
            your orders.

BRAGEN: Guards... Guards!

QUINN: Dead! The Daleks have killed them. You still have
            your guard units in the interior. How long will it take
            them to get here?

BRAGEN: That depends.

QUINN: Well, get them!

BRAGEN: They will be intercepted by the Daleks.

QUINN: Exactly! It will draw them away from here and give
            the Doctor a chance to deal with them.

BRAGEN: I refuse to allow my guards to be sacrificed.

QUINN: In that case the Daleks will destroy everything on this
            colony.

            *(BRAGEN struggles with himself for a moment, then
            speaks into the intercom.)*

BRAGEN: Guards. This is Bragen speaking. All units will report
            immediately to the capital. Be prepared to face the
            rebel Daleks.

(He turns off the intercom.)

There. Are you satisfied?

QUINN: I hope it works.

29. *LESTERSON'S LABORATORY.*

(THE DOCTOR peers into the laboratory and signals for VALMAR to follow him. BEN and POLLY emerge from their hiding place.)

THE DOCTOR : Ben! Polly!

BEN: Did you hear what Bragen said?

THE DOCTOR: Yes, I did.

BEN: Well I only hope the Daleks do go for the guards.

POLLY: A lot of the Daleks went out just now.

THE DOCTOR: Good... because we're going inside. Come on Valmar.

(THE DOCTOR moves away. BEN and POLLY look at each other in horror as THE DOCTOR enters the capsule. He quickly emerges again, bringing with him a grey junction box. It has a number of cables plugged into it.)

Ben, give me that... that cable over there... Polly, keep watch at the door.

(BEN picks up a cable from a pile of them in the corner. Each of the cables has a plug attached to it. THE DOCTOR removes a cable from one of the sockets, as though unsure of which one to take out. He puts it over the console. BEN brings over his cable. THE DOCTOR plugs it into the empty socket

and flinches as though expecting an explosion.
Nothing happens and he looks puzzled.)

BEN: D'you know what you're doing?

THE DOCTOR: Of course I do!

                (THE DOCTOR *answers forcefully, looks down at the*
                box in puzzlement, and then looks up at VALMAR.
                VALMAR *takes the junction box and replaces it inside*
                the capsule. THE DOCTOR *and* BEN *start to unwind the*
                cable that THE DOCTOR *has just plugged in.* VALMAR
                comes back out of the capsule.)

BEN: Why can't you just take all the plugs out and cut the
                power off?

THE DOCTOR: Because I prefer to do it my way.

POLLY: Look out!

                (They all duck down as a DALEK *enters the labora-*
                tory. A SECOND DALEK *comes out of the capsule.)*

SECOND DALEK: Sta-tic po-wer is be-ing stored. We can dis-man-tle
                the hu-man el-ect-ric sys-tem.

FIRST DALEK: The law of the Da-leks is in force.

SECOND DALEK: Ex-ter-min-at-ion of hu-mans.

                (THE DOCTOR *edges round the side of the bench.)*

FIRST DALEK: Our ca-bles have been moved.

                (The two DALEKS *follow the cable towards the*
                bench... and to THE DOCTOR, *who is holding the*
                other end! As they are about to discover THE DOC-
                TOR, LESTERSON *stands up.)*

LESTERSON: I could tell you who did it!

FIRST DALEK: What were you doing in there?

LESTERSON: I want to help you.

DALEK: Why?

> *(THE DOCTOR signals to POLLY and BEN to keep hidden and, whilst the DALEKS are occupied with LESTERSON, he starts to move towards the main switch.)*

LESTERSON: I am your ser... vant.

FIRST DALEK: We do not need hu-mans now.

LESTERSON: Ah, but... but you wouldn't kill me. I gave you life.

FIRST DALEK: Yes, you gave us life.

> *(The DALEK callously exterminates LESTERSON. THE DOCTOR turns, horrified, and then continues to plug in the cable. Again he reacts as if he is expecting something to happen immediately... it doesn't. He adjusts a dial on the generator and turns expectantly towards the DALEKS. Still nothing happens. He turns back and starts to pull switches all over the place. The DALEKS discover VALMAR. He makes a dash for the door and flings himself out as the DALEKS fire. He escapes. BEN drags POLLY down to the ground. THE DOCTOR pulls another switch. There is a loud explosion and THE DOCTOR is flung to the ground. The two DALEKS immediately swing around crazily, lights flashing from within them and smoke bursting out from their casing. One of the DALEKS explodes, flame shooting out from within. Another DALEK smashes against a wall. Two more crash into each other, smoke pouring out of both of them.)*

Ex-ter-min-aaaaaagh!

30. INTERIOR THE CAPSULE.

(DALEKS are still coming off the conveyor belt, but now smoke is billowing from them as they move through the arches. One of the DALEKS hits a pillar, which starts to collapse.)

DALEK: Ex-ter-min-aaaaaaate. Aaaaaagh! Out of con-trol! Out of con-trol!

31. THE GOVERNOR'S TERRACE ROOM.

(QUINN and BRAGEN stare in surprise at the DALEK that is in the room. It has stopped moving and a trickle of smoke issues from within it, its various sticks all pointing downwards.)

BRAGEN: What's happened to it?

QUINN: I don't know...

BRAGEN: It seems your friend, the Examiner, was successful after all.

(BRAGEN takes advantage of the situation and chops his hand down on QUINN's gun hand. The gun clatters to the floor. BRAGEN hits QUINN and, before he can recover, BRAGEN seizes the gun. He aims it at QUINN's head.)

Now I shall restore law and order on this planet.

QUINN: Not your law, Bragen. That's finished for good.

BRAGEN: You'll obey me, or...

QUINN: Your day is over, Bragen. No-one will obey you now.

BRAGEN: I am still the Governor...

(He levels the gun and aims it at QUINN.)

...and you will...

(There is a shot. BRAGEN *is hit. He drops the gun and turns round in surprise to see* VALMAR *standing there, gun in hand.)*

Valmar...

*(*BRAGEN *falls to the ground, dead.)*

VALMAR: He was a murderer.

(He tosses the gun away.)

Enough of guns. There is a lot of clearing up to be done.

QUINN: We will rebuild together. What is the extent of the damage?

VALMAR: I don't know if it's repairable. The whole electrical system...

*(*QUINN *and* VALMAR *leave the room.)*

32. LESTERSON'S LABORATORY.

*(*BEN *and* POLLY *are standing over* THE DOCTOR*'s semi-conscious body.* QUINN *and* VALMAR *come in.)*

QUINN: Is he all right?

BEN: Oh he's okay... he's knocked himself out.

*(*THE DOCTOR *quickly comes to. His initial fearful expression quickly changes to an inane grin as soon as he sees that* POLLY *and* BEN *are both safe.)*

QUINN: It was a miracle. How did you do it?

THE DOCTOR: Eh. What happened?

(He looks behind him and gingerly feels the back of his sore head.)

Ouch! What did I do, what did I do?

BEN: You destroyed the Daleks, that's what you did!

POLLY: No need to be modest about it.

(THE DOCTOR looks round the room, noticing for the first time what has happened to the DALEKS.)

THE DOCTOR: Did I do that?

POLLY: You know you did!

VALMAR: You used the power from the colony's electric supply... overfed it... and blew up their temporary static circuit. Well didn't you?

THE DOCTOR: Did I do all that?

(He practically rubs his hands with glee.)

VALMAR: You may have stopped the Daleks, but have you any idea of the damage you've done to the colony?

THE DOCTOR: Oh... er, there was a blow back, was there?

VALMAR: A blow back? Our power supply has been destroyed! It'll be months before we can get things back to normal.

QUINN: Valmar!

THE DOCTOR: That is unfortunate.

(His gleeful expression is instantly replaced by a hangdog look.)

VALMAR: But did it have to be this way?

THE DOCTOR: Did a lot of damage, did I? Come on, I think we'd better get out of here... before they send us the bill.

(VALMAR *and* QUINN *move into the capsule to review the damage.* THE DOCTOR *nods towards the laboratory door and the three travellers exit.*)

33. THE MERCURY SWAMP.

(BEN *and* POLLY *pick their way across the swamp.* THE DOCTOR *follows behind, once again playing his recorder.*)

BEN: Well, I mean I didn't expect a brass band to be playing, but I wouldn't have thought a 'thank you' would have hurt anybody.

POLLY: But Ben, think of all those poor people... all killed.

BEN: I know, but the Doctor saved the colony from being completely wiped out.

POLLY: Hmm.

BEN: Yeah, and he was telling them all along, but would they listen?

POLLY: Mind you, he wasn't very convincing when he was trying to explain it to Valmar and Quinn and everybody.

BEN: No, he wasn't, was he?

(*A slight doubt crosses their minds. They pause and wait for* THE DOCTOR *to catch up. He stands between them, playing the recorder. He looks at each of them in turn, and takes the recorder from his lips.*)

POLLY: Doctor? You did know what you were doing, didn't you?

(THE DOCTOR *looks at* POLLY *and* BEN *very solemnly, then suddenly chuckles to himself and gives a tremendous wink. As they reach the TARDIS, they see a* DALEK *standing nearby, dead and lifeless.* THE DOCTOR *edges past it and enters the TARDIS.* BEN *laughs and follows him in, slapping the* DALEK *as he passes.*)

BEN: Oh, you needn't worry about them anymore, Doctor. Just a heap of old iron now.

(POLLY *grimaces at the* DALEK *and enters the TARDIS. For a moment there is silence, then a familiar grating sound starts to echo across the swamp and the TARDIS starts to dematerialize. As it fades from view, the* DALEK'S *eye-stick weakly rises up to follow it.*)

THE TRIBE OF GUM
Anthony Coburn
Edited by John McElroy

THE DAEMONS
Robert Sloman and Barry Letts
Edited by John McElroy

THE MASTERS OF LUXOR

THE TOMB OF THE CYBERMEN
Gerry Davis and Kit Pedler
Edited by John McElroy